WOMEN AT THE WELL

Published by LIFE Publishing
P.O. Box 982000, Fort Worth, Texas 76182.

ISBN 0-9653940-1-8

Printed in the United States of America
First Printing: April 2001.

WOMEN AT THE WELL

31 Refreshing Devotions
for every facet of a woman's life

CONTENTS

INTRODUCTION

I love to rise early and have my quiet, secluded time with the Lord. I have learned to pause and listen to what He wants to say to me as I place before Him all my needs and burdens for others in prayer. I find a fulfillment in my whole being, and I feel prepared to meet the challenges of my day.

If we want relationships that go beyond the surface with our family and loved ones, it is vital that we maintain good communication. In the same way, we must set aside time to fellowship with the Lord if we want to draw from the well of His wisdom and love. I hope this devotional will encourage and help you in having that special time of intimate communication between you and the Lord.

"Women at the Well" contains personal insights from myself as well as my dear friends and guests on our LIFE TODAY television program. In these pages, you will find inspiration to equip you for any circumstance in life. We were created with three aspects of our being: *spirit, soul and body.*

The *spirit* is our invisible nature or what we truly are. The *soul* is our individual and essential being. It has three basic functions: the mind, the will and the emotions. The third aspect is the *body*, our physical housing of the other two. I believe that these three aspects of a woman's life are so intricately woven that if one is out of balance it will affect the others.

I receive living water from my quiet times with the Lord; it helps me balance my spirit, soul and body. I let my "roots grow down deep into Him," and my mind gets renewed to see His perspective of everything that pertains to life.

When the Holy Spirit is in control, I interact in my other relationships with love, joy, peace, patience, kindness, goodness, faithfulness, gentleness and self-control. (Galatians 6:22-23) These are the byproducts of my special time of fellowship with Him. I get energized by the Holy Spirit, and the very character and nature of Christ begins to grow and be evidenced in my life.

I love the way the New Living translation interprets this Scripture in Colossians 2:6-7. *And now just as you have accepted Christ Jesus as your Lord, you must continue to live in obedience to him. Let your roots grow down into Him and draw up nourishment from Him so you will grow in faith, strong and vigorous in the truth you were taught. Let your lives overflow with thanksgiving for all He has done.*

Satan's driving ambition is to disconnect our lifeline to Jesus. He has many deceptive devices, and if we allow him to get his foot in the door of our lives, we can quickly become his victims. His oppression and darkness can sweep over our spirit, our soul and even our body.

Paul's letter to the Colossian Christians offers us valuable insight in guarding against satan's deception. (Colossians 2:8-10) *Don't let anyone lead you astray with empty philosophy and high-sounding nonsense that come from human thinking and from the evil powers of this world ... For in Christ, the fullness of God lives in a human body, and you are complete through your union with Christ. He is the Lord over every ruler and authority in the universe.* (NLT)

Through some difficult life-experiences and through studying scripture, I am continually learning how to be alert and recognize the deception of satan in my life. That awareness has given me a passionate sense of responsibility to keep the pathway cleared in all three areas — to be complete in my spirit, soul and body.

I am discovering how our fellowship can take on a new dimension when we commit our lives and submit our wills to Christ. (Romans 12:1-2) We must seek to learn from Him, His life and His teachings. Daily, we must recognize and ask for the Holy Spirit's fullness and power. In total dependence and in vital union with Him, we will have everything we need in our spirit, soul and body for each day that He gives us to serve Him. You will be filled to overflowing as you draw from "Women at the Well" and experience the power and love of a living God who cares about every area of your life. *Betty Robison*

PART ONE: SPIRIT

Betty
Robison

Betty co-hosts the LIFE

TODAY show with her

husband, James Robison.

She is the mother of three

children and the grand-

mother of eleven. She has

been married for over thirty-

eight years and resides in the

Dallas-Fort Worth area.

THE CRUSHING AND BUILDING OF MY SPIRIT

James has often described our younger daughter, Robin, as "high energy," "strong spirited," and "determined to the end." Even now, as a wife and mother of three, we are amazed at Robin's creative drive to organize her family and household to live in the fullness of God's plan.

When Robin was eleven years old, she taught us all an incredible lesson of faith. An unsightly tumor began to grow on the left side of her bottom lip. James and I were immediately concerned and had our family doctor examine it. He felt it was not dangerous, but encouraged us to have a specialist remove it. I was so disappointed when the specialist told us that he would not be able to schedule the procedure for weeks. After we left the doctor's office, Robin decided that the delay was a sign that

God was going to heal her miraculously.

I was amazed and surprised by Robin's faith. Even though our family had been learning to trust God for miracles and healing in our personal lives and ministry, I was taken aback by my young daughter's resolve.

Extended family and close friends were encouraged by Robin's faith and joined us in praying for healing. I, too, had studied God's Word and believed that He still healed people super-naturally. I knew I could trust Him for healing in my own body and for others. Yet, when my own children are suffering, I tend to want Him to fix everything, and fast!

I prayed day and night for Robin's healing, but as the weeks went by, my faith began to falter. Every time I looked at that grotesque tumor on my beautiful daughter's lip, my heart ached. Robin, however, went through her days as if the tumor didn't exist. Her faith was incredible! I didn't want to discourage her, so when I was having a "low moment," I would go off to my closet, shut the door, and cry out to God in desperation.

To make matters worse, Robin's school had a special program scheduled, and she had a significant part to perform. She was confident that the tumor would be gone by then. The week before the school program, I began putting intense pressure on God to "Do something!" because I couldn't stand it any longer. That night I went to bed very discouraged. As my restlessness gave way to sleep, I found myself in the midst of a dream that was so real that I perceived it to be a word from God. In the dream, I saw Robin coming into our bedroom holding the tumor in her hand.

The next morning, I eagerly rushed into Robin's room, hoping to see that the tumor was gone. It wasn't. I was heartbroken, but I still shared my dream with Robin. Her excitement about my dream moved her to an even higher level of faith. Later that day, as I walked past her bedroom door, I heard Robin talking aloud. I called through the door, "Honey, who are you talking to?" Robin answered, "I'm practicing my testimony so I'll know just what to say when God heals me." I smiled bravely and made a quick exit so that she would not see me cry.

A few days later, as James was preparing to leave town for a meeting, he said, "Betty, I feel that God wants us to pray a very specific prayer about that tumor. I think Robin and I need to trust God to heal her by this Friday." This was only a few days away. I admired Robin and James's big step of faith, and I begged God to come through for my daughter.

On Friday morning, Robin was awakened by her hand slapping her face, right on her bottom lip, where the tumor was. When she opened her eyes, she saw what she perceived to be an angel, kneeling by her bedside. As Robin got up, she saw something lying on the sheets. It was the tumor. She quickly looked into the mirror and saw only a tiny red spot on her lip where the tumor had been. She ran into my room shouting, "Mom, it's gone! It's gone!" as she showed me the tumor in her hand.

"Oh, Jesus, thank you!" I rejoiced. Robin was healed just in time for the school program, and she testified before the whole school about her special miracle from God.

Words of Life

Whoever then humbles himself as this child, he is the greatest in the kingdom of heaven. And whoever receives one such child in My name receives Me. (Matthew 18:4-5) Then some children were brought to Him so that He might lay His hands on them and pray; and the disciples rebuked them. But Jesus said, "Let the children alone, and do not hinder them from coming to Me; for the kingdom of heaven belongs to such as these." (Matthew 19:13-14)

Living It Out

When you're faced with a difficult or seemingly impossible situation, remind yourself of the faith of a child. Children trust their parents to make the best choices on their behalf. In the same way, God's intervention, whether through supernatural or natural means, is always in our best interest. Make a decision today to fill your heart with faith that He will come through—one way or another—one day or another.

Drawing From the Well of Prayer

Dear Lord, thank You for Your Word and Your Spirit that grows us in faith and in the under-standing of the greatness of Your power. Help me to trust and obey You as You carry me through dark and difficult paths. Let my spirit soar to high places with You. Comfort me with Your nearness and speak tender words of love in my ears.

Stormie Omartian

Stormie is an award-winning singer/songwriter and the author of numerous books, including, *The Power of a Praying Wife, Stormie, Just Enough Light for the Step I'm On* and *Greater Health God's Way*. She and her husband, Michael, have been married for more than twenty-seven years and have three grown children.

STANDING STRONG

"Stormie," the voice on the other end of the line sounded uncharacteristically small and shaken.

"What did the doctor say?"

"It's not good—" her voice broke.

"What do you mean?"

"The cancer is back."

I had met Diane in drama class in high school twenty-eight years before; we were best friends. The bad news came in June, and by September she went home to be with her heavenly Father.

In the months after Diane's death, I had a hysterectomy; we sold our house and business, moved to a new location and built a new studio. Then an unforeseen turn of events in the music business put us under severe financial strain, which in turn inflicted tremendous strain on our marriage. I became physically and emotionally drained.

"God, it feels as if my life is coming to an end," I cried to the Lord. "What can replace these losses? All this is overwhelming, Lord, and I can't handle it anymore."

"Good. Now let Me take this burden for you," I heard the Lord instruct my heart. "You just stand strong in all you know of My truth, and I will take care of everything."

I stayed in the Word, I prayed, I praised, I surrendered more of myself and my life to Him, I lived God's way even when I felt like giving up.

I learned that God is God when things are bad as well as when they are good and when it is dark as well as when it is light. Sometimes the darkness around us is not a darkness of death but rather a darkness like the womb, where we are growing and being made ready for birth. There are certain valuable experiences in the Lord that can only be found in the dark times.

Eventually things turned around. I received deliverance from my grief over Diane's death as God gave me deeper relationships with others and with Him. I recovered from the hysterectomy and felt better than I had in years. Our studio and house were saved, and our marriage became stronger than ever.

I knew things could have easily gone the other way. My life could have been washed away by bankruptcy, divorce, and emotional and physical sickness. These kinds of things happen to good people all the time. But I hung on to the Lord, and not only did I get through it, I came out stronger. *The key was standing strong in Him and doing what was right, no matter what.*

I learned that there comes a point in life when we've had enough teaching, enough counseling, enough deliverance, and enough knowledge of God's ways to be able to stand on our own two feet and say, "I am not going to live on the negative side of life any more." We have to decide we won't be the victims of our circumstances. We are to stand strong in Him.

Don't be frightened if you are doing everything you know to do and things are going well, and then suddenly depression will cloud your mind or low self-esteem will dominate your actions. Or unforgiveness will return in full force, or all hell will break loose in a relationship. This means you are under an attack from the devil. At those times you have to understand without a doubt that when you walk with Jesus, you never walk backwards. If we have our eyes on Him we will go from glory to glory and strength to strength.

And finally, there will be times when your prayers are not answered—at least not exactly the way you prayed them or according to your timetable. If that happens, trust that God knows what is best. Unanswered prayer reveals two things: God's grace and power. His grace to sustain and keep you, and His power to deliver you. He wants us to see that *we are limited* in our power and *He is not.*

Words of Life

Many are the afflictions of the righteous; But the Lord delivers him out of them all. (Psalm 34:19) 🌸 Beloved, do not be surprised at the fiery ordeal among you, which comes upon you for your testing, as though some strange thing were happening to you; but to the degree that you share the sufferings of Christ, keep on rejoicing; so that also at the revelation of His glory, you may rejoice with exultation. (1 Peter 4:12-13) ❊ Be on the alert, stand firm in the faith, act like men, be strong. (1 Corinthians 16:13)

Living It Out

Years ago our pastor instructed each family to go out and find a rock large enough to write the words, "As for me and my house, we will serve the Lord" (Joshua 24:15), and then put it in a prominent place in their home. Michael and I placed our stone next to the fireplace, and every time we see it we remember our commitment to serve God and stand strong in Him. I believe the devil knows it's there too.

Go find yourself a decent-sized rock, print that Scripture on it and place it in the heart of your home. Whether you live in a trailer, a mansion, or a corner of someone else's apartment, it's a scriptural proclamation of where you stand, and it helps you to stand taller in the presence of the giants of adversity.

Drawing From the Well of Prayer

Lord, give me Your strength and Your perspective when my way becomes clouded with uncertainty and pain. Help me to stand strong, being certain that You are at work on my behalf— molding my heart and orchestrating my circumstances.

Esther Burroughs

Esther is a lyricist of eight musicals with her composer husband, Bob Burroughs. She has written many magazine articles and books which include: *Empowered*, *A Garden Path to Mentoring* and *Splash the Living Water*. She speaks at women's conferences.

EMBRACING INTERRUPTIONS

I had a schedule to keep as usual, but in spite of myself I hollered across the driveway: "May I help?"

"I'm trying to get a stationary bike from my car trunk to the upstairs bedroom," the young woman replied.

Not knowing this neighbor very well, I inquired what she did. She told me that she worked in a professional office in downtown Atlanta. Then it was her turn. She had seen the taxi come to my doorstep and had seen suitcases very often and wondered what I did.

"I travel and speak to women about prayer and its influence in everyday living."

Without asking about prayer or how I teach, she said, "Oh, would you pray for me?"

"I'd be honored. How can I pray for you?"

Her emptiness and thirst came flooding out. "I'm a newlywed. We are quite wealthy. Well," she continued, "I was wealthy. I didn't know I had married a man who is an addictive gambler. He has lost everything I had and has now walked out on our marriage."

My heart sank. That "still small voice" had tried to interrupt me six months earlier about her need.

You and I live and breathe by our organizers and calendars—while Jesus lived each interruption as God's divine appointment. Think about that: living daily to expect an interruption as a divine appointment with God. Regarding circumstances in our lives, we perhaps are quick to say, "What a coincidence." Or "You won't believe what happened!" Jesus was never surprised by the activity of God. In fact, He only did what the Father told Him to do.

In Matthew, chapter 8, Jesus was interrupted eleven times. Each interruption met the needs of the people, showed His power, and displayed God's glory. He kept stopping along the way, embracing the interruptions, so that He could minister, heal and offer eternal life. What an example! Consider living in the expectancy of interruptions turned into divine encounters.

For example, here's a typical day for me:

I'm up early for my quiet time, which may be interrupted by a phone call from my husband about a matter that needs prayer.

I drop off a wedding invitation to be framed as a gift. I want it to be a prayer blessing for this young couple as they start married life.

Then, perhaps, on to the bank to make a deposit. The clerk says, "Have a good day!" My response is "God bless your day!"

My next stop is the grocery store. As I punch the debit card machine button, the young clerk comments on the much-needed rain in Florida. I respond, "It is an answer to prayer, for sure." She smiles widely and nods. Our hearts have a knowing exchange.

I go home and take a nap. Refreshed, I sit down at my computer to continue writing. A fax comes with another ministry opportunity, which causes me to give thanks for God's faithfulness. I stop to fax a copy to my assistant.

I strive to emulate Jesus' attitude in Matthew 8. Not once does Jesus inquire about the time of day or complain about all the encounters He has experienced. I want the Holy Spirit to allow the flow of living water to splash out on the people I encounter and to draw others to the well. I want to embrace interruptions like the Master did!

Words of Life

Now on the last day, the great day of the feast, Jesus stood and cried out, saying, "If anyone is thirsty, let him come to Me and drink. He who believes in Me, as the Scripture said, 'From his innermost being shall flow rivers of living water.'" (John 7:37-38) ❦ I can do nothing on My own initiative. As I hear, I judge; and My judgment is just, because I do not seek My own will, but the will of Him who sent Me. (John 5:30) Additional Reading: John 15:1-16

Living It Out

Practice going out of your way, on your way. Be on the lookout to bless people with your words and actions, especially when they show up unexpectedly in your day. Embrace interruptions like Jesus did. His focus was one thing: doing His Father's will every moment of His life on earth.

Drawing From the Well of Prayer

Father, please develop a willingness within me to go out of my way as I go through my day to bless others. Help me not to be irritated by interruptions, but rather to embrace them as divine appointments straight from Your hand.

Thelma Wells

Thelma is one of the keynote speakers for the popular *Women of Faith* conferences. A business professional and keynote speaker, Thelma is also the founder/president of A Woman of God Ministries, Dallas, Texas. She is the recipient of numerous awards and is the author of several books, including, *Bumblebee Fly Anyway— Defying the Odds*, *God Will Make a Way* and *We Brake for Joy*.

WHAT GOD ORDAINS, HE SUSTAINS

Contemplating whether or not to quit my banking job and go into business for myself was a frightening dilemma. I had moved up rapidly at NorthPark National Bank, a beautiful bank in a prestigious section of Dallas. An attorney and I had written a manual that was considered to be "the last word in new accounts" and was distributed throughout the state of Texas. In addition, I received accolades for my teaching with the American Institute of Banking.

While teaching banking classes, I developed a short seminar about how people could become the best of whatever they wanted to be. People began asking me to come to their banks, organizations and churches to deliver that motivational speech.

At the same time, people were inviting me to conduct

training sessions on subjects I didn't know anything about. Once a group was serious about hiring me to speak, I would spend hours, including many sleepless nights, to develop a seminar on that subject.

The idea to quit my job and go into the professional speaking business full-time weighed heavily on my mind. However, after working at the bank for ten years, I had status, authority, a paycheck and other perks and benefits. Writing my resignation wouldn't be easy. But the passion of my heart to be a professional speaker spoke louder than my fear. I'd known for some time that what I really wanted out of life was to help people be better people. It was time to go!

Just to make sure, I sought the opinion of someone who lived for the Lord and who would give me her honest perspective on my thinking process. I called my husband's Aunt Doretha. She asked me, "Have you talked to the Lord and your husband about this?" I answered a resounding "Yes!" Aunt Doretha then proceeded to give the best philosophical and theological thesis of anyone I had paid attention to in a long time. She said:

"If God said do it, you do it. What God ordains, He sustains. Step on out there in faith, Baby. Everything we do is in faith whether we know it or not. What do you have to lose if you're doing it for God and He gets the glory?"

With that final blast of encouragement, I stepped out on faith and became a training consultant. My first large contract was for the very bank that I had resigned from. God financed my business without my having to borrow a single penny.

These past years as a full-time professional speaker have not been without trial and error, loss and aggravation, heartache and tears. But the good times far outweigh the bad.

If you are facing a frightening decision in some area of your life, be assured that God knows all about the situation. He also has a solution for you. Ask Him for wisdom. I have discovered that God places ideas in our minds for a reason: He has a plan for each of us, and He provides the time, resources and people to help us reach our heartfelt goals.

If you are obedient to God's Word and are committed to fulfilling His plans for your life, you can face the human fears of decision making with the assurance that God is in control of the situation.

Words of Life

"Then you will call upon Me and come and pray to Me, and I will listen to you. You will seek Me and find Me, when you search for me with all your heart." (Jeremiah 29:12-13) 🌸 For I am the Lord your God, Who upholds your right hand, Who says to you, "Do not fear, I will help you." (Isaiah 41:13) 🌸 For the vision is yet for the appointed time; it hastens toward the goal, and it will not fail. Though it tarries, wait for it; for it will certainly come, it will not delay. (Habakkuk 2:3)

Living It Out

The next time you find yourself facing a difficult dilemma,

try Dr. Viktor Frankl's method of dealing with fear:

1. Write down the dilemma.

2. Write down all the advantages and disadvantages.

3. Determine the worst-case scenario.

4. Ask yourself, "What difference will it make

   in one to five years?"

And finally, consider this definition of failure: Failure is

never trying to do what is in your heart to do. Psalm 37 reminds

us that when we live for God and want to be in His perfect will,

He places desires in our hearts that are designed to help us carry

out His will more fully.

Drawing From the Well of Prayer

Lord, You know my

purpose in life and how

my experiences build

wisdom and faith for

future challenges. When

I become fearful of the

future, please remind me

that You are sufficient in

everything. You are in

control. It's great to realize

that I'm not out here

making decisions alone.

May that blessed assurance

make me act boldly, even

when I feel afraid.

Lisa Bevere

Lisa is a best-selling author, popular speaker, and radio and television guest. Her books include: *Out of Control and Loving It, The True Measure of a Woman, You Are Not What You Weigh and Be Angry But Don't Blow It!* She lives in Colorado with her husband, John, also a best-selling author, and their four sons.

FREEDOM FROM "SELF"

One day while I was in a tired, frazzled, quite unattractive state, I looked at myself in the mirror and heard the Lord tell me, "You are not who you see." I argued, "I am *too* who I see!" He explained, "It may be true that you feel tired, stressed, worn out, or fat, but that is not the truth about who you are. When you become empowered with the truth, then you can make decisions to leave the past behind and walk free from bondage to the image you have of yourself."

The Lord began to show me that the image I had of myself was who I became—not outwardly, but inwardly. My desire to conform to the world's image of "the perfect woman," my longing for the approval of our culture, and gauging my success or failure according to the messages I received from the world's idols only led to inward bondage.

It's easy to exchange God's view of "the perfect woman" for the world's view. Almost without exception, the covers of secular women's magazines boast young, seductive women and promise to reveal the secrets to great sex, ageless beauty and thinner thighs. The ultimate goal is self-gratification.

God wants us to strip away the veil of self-worship. You may argue, "How could I worship myself? I have a bad self-image!" I would answer, "Whenever you are limited by your self-image, then the image of self becomes your master."

God doesn't want us fulfilled through self; He wants us fulfilled through Him. The Word of God is set up to reveal to us a good *God*. To feel good about ourselves, *we* have to be good.

Self-image is the defense mechanism we project while trying to protect who we really are. It's the projected image versus the protected one. Self-image is the image left vulnerable when we lose the innocence of self-*un*awareness.

Most of us lose the unconscious sense of our physical body and instead become tethered to a consciousness of our body that makes us feel uncomfortable. *To lose consciousness of one's self happens when we become more aware of God and His will than we are of self and our will.* This is a work of the Spirit, accomplished as we begin to renounce our natural limitations and abandon ourselves to Him.

God doesn't want us to seek fulfillment through the avenue of self—that's futile and destructive. He wants us to seek fulfillment in Him by seeking and serving Him and others. When we shift our focus from self to Savior, we will experience an ongoing heart-level transformation into His image.

Most Christian women want to be like the world but not part of it. God said in Ezekiel, "You long with your eyes and with your heart, and you broke my heart with your adultery." God wants to set us free from coveting what the world dictates as ideal. And that begins with an inward transformation that leads to freedom from the tyranny of self.

Words of Life

For You formed my inward parts; You wove me in my mother's womb. I will give thanks to You, for I am fearfully and wonderfully made; Wonderful are Your works, And my soul knows it very well. (Psalm 139:13-14) But we all, with unveiled face, beholding as in a mirror the glory of the Lord, are being transformed into the same image from glory to glory, just as from the Lord, the Spirit. (2 Corinthians 3:18) It was for freedom that Christ set us free; therefore keep standing firm and do not be subject again to a yoke of slavery. (Galatians 5:1)

Living It Out

Guard yourself against allowing the images from magazines, billboards and television to make you self-aware. Choose to believe God's truth about you. Look deeply into the loving eyes of the Lord and let Him transform your mind and heart into His image. Don't let a bad self-image keep you from fulfilling your goals and destiny.

Drawing From the Well of Prayer

Dear Father, I want to be free and have the "unawareness" of a child again. Turn my focus away from me and toward You. Draw me close that I may see Your face and feel Your loving arms. Help me tear down the idol of self and in its place build an altar to You.

Ann Pretorius

Ann is the co-founder of Jesus Alive! Ministries which carries out relief projects in war-torn, drought-stricken Africa. Through a partnership with LIFE Outreach, Ann and her husband, Peter, have also founded several orphanages in Africa and have conducted water-drilling operations. Their ministry is based out of Johannesburg, South Africa.

FORGIVING GRACE

Early one morning, the telephone rang. It was my older sister with devastating news. My youngest sister, Teri, and her husband, Jay, had been murdered. My four-year-old nephew and twenty-one-month-old niece were now orphans, and our entire family was thrust into the news spotlight because the murderer was a notorious serial killer.

Having heard of similar tragedies across our native South Africa, I often wondered how people coped with such cruel circumstances. Since my husband, Peter, and I had given up our business to start a ministry to our country's impoverished black people, I often prayed that serving others would shield us from such evil.

As my sister's shocking message replayed in my head,

I began to cry out to God. Instantly, I felt God's power come upon me and I had a strong urge to pray: "Father, forgive him; he did not know what he was doing." As those words came out of my mouth, I became aware of a river of forgiveness flowing out of my spirit.

Feelings of hatred, anger and unforgiveness toward this man, who had taken the precious lives of my loved ones, threatened to overtake my emotions—but the strength of the river would not let these feelings take root. The flow of God's forgiving grace was obliterating them.

My initial experience with God's forgiving grace was with my own sin. I had asked Him to forgive me in a prayer of salvation and He extended His mercy to me. I had memorized the Lord's Prayer and understood that I must forgive others' trespasses against me, as I am forgiven of my trespasses. But when faced with this seemingly impossible task of forgiving the man who killed my family members, my greatest inspiration came from Jesus Himself. He extended mercy to cruel, godless men—even as he was dying from the terrible wounds inflicted by those men.

Another source of inspiration for me was realizing that the Father sacrificed His own son to offer forgiveness to a degraded, dying world—and to sinners like me. He knew His unfathomable act of grace could empower us to face any crisis in life … if we would open our hearts to receive it.

I could have so easily become embittered toward the native South African people after what happened to my sister's family. I could have abandoned the evangelistic and humanitarian relief work that my husband and I had begun, but God did a supernatural healing within me. I forgave and let God's indescribable comfort absorb the shock and pain of losing Teri and Jay.

Instead of "returning evil for evil," my husband and I increased our work of "blessing." Today, our ministry, Jesus Alive!, reaches millions of people in twelve countries within Sub-Saharan Africa. We take food, water, clothing and medical supplies to these impoverished and war-torn countries. We establish agriculture projects, drill water wells and build schools, but most of all, we take the transforming message of God's love and forgiveness to hurting people.

Words of Life

To sum up, let all be harmonious, sympathetic, brotherly, kindhearted, and humble in spirit; not returning evil for evil, or insult for insult, but giving a blessing instead; for you were called for the very purpose that you might inherit a blessing. (1 Peter 3:8-10) Never take your own revenge, beloved, but leave room for the wrath of God, for it is written, "Vengeance is Mine, I will repay," says the Lord. "But if your enemy is hungry, feed him, and if he is thirsty, give him a drink; for in so doing you will heap burning coals upon his head." Do not be overcome by evil, but overcome evil with good. (Romans 12:19-21) Get rid of all bitterness, rage and anger, brawling and slander, along with every form of malice. Be kind and compassionate to one another, forgiving each other, just as in Christ God forgave you. (Ephesians 4:31-5:1)

Living It Out

If you are faced with a dark situation or season and your emotions threaten to overtake you, realize there is a river of God's grace that flows down to you. Cry out to Him, believing that He will supply what is needed to sustain you. God has enough love and grace to surround you and hold you. He has a plan to comfort and strengthen you. He wants you to know Him intimately. You cannot do this in your own strength, but God has the power ... and He desires to give it to you.

Drawing From the Well of Prayer

Father, empower me to forgive others as freely as You have forgiven me. I recognize that I cannot do this on my own. You will have to do it through me by the power of Your Holy Spirit. I open myself to You. Come and fill me with Your love and grace.

Jeanne Rogers

Jeanne has worked with James and Betty Robison in music ministry for over 30 years. She has produced a number of worship cassettes and CDs, and is a writer. Jeanne and her husband, Jim Rogers, executive vice president of LIFE Outreach, have three children.

No Substitute For God's Plan

I had received many personal promises from the Lord preparing me to be a worship leader over a five-year span. Music was my passion, and I was excited, yet scared, as I prepared to enter a new season of ministry. I learned a difficult lesson on my very first opportunity to lead worship.

The small conference would take me to another state, far from my familiar and supportive surroundings. For twenty years, I had been a featured soloist for James Robison's large crusades across the U.S. and never experienced any fear in that role. However, this particular conference would be hosting men and women from a conservative denomination, and I was concerned about how they would respond to a more intimate style of worship than what they were accustomed to. God had been assuring me with glorious promises and visions of the good things that would happen if I obeyed His call to use my voice for Him. But now that the opportunity had finally arrived, I was terrified!

I was told that I could bring whatever keyboard player that I wanted. I called Kirk Dearman, a well-known worship leader and songwriter. He agreed to play, sing and even bring his talented wife, Debbie, to sing and assist me in my first experience leading worship.

We planned our music, rehearsed and traveled together to the conference. Kirk had no idea that I was so afraid. I was secretly planning to let him take the lead on the first service and I thought if I felt confident, I might step into the leadership role later in the week. However, God's "perfect plan" began to unfold early the first morning of the conference.

"Jeanne?" the voice on the phone sounded worried.

"Yes."

"This is Debbie. Kirk is really sick this morning."

"What's wrong?"

"His temperature is 105 degrees, and he's lost his voice."

As I hung up the phone, I felt God's finger shaking in my face. He was saying, "You thought you could slip this one by me, didn't you? Now I have taken away your substitutes and your crutches. You will have to trust me."

He was right; I was cornered. Now I would have to lead worship by myself, and I would have to do it without any instruments! I fell to my knees and asked God to give me the faith to lead His people to encounter Him.

I stepped onto the platform of the church that morning, and God poured down His anointing in a way that I have not experienced since. At one point, we knelt in worship, afraid to move or speak. We were being held—suspended under the weight of God's glory. An incredibly long and peaceful silence filled the room, and we just basked in the presence of God.

I've been in some very powerful services since that time, but I have never led in a service that could compare to that first, desperate experience. That humble beginning launched me into my destiny. I didn't know it at the time, but I would stand before a gathering of ten thousand believers in my next conference at James Robison's Bible Conference in Dallas. Many large conferences would follow over a period of ten years.

God was merciful to teach me to stop looking for a substitute and simply obey Him. I learned that He can be trusted to equip us to walk the path that He has charted. He gives us precious promises and the power of the Holy Spirit to guide us when we choose to follow His plan.

Words of Life

And do not be conformed to this world, but be transformed by the renewing of your mind, so that you may prove what the will of God is, that which is good and acceptable and perfect. (Romans 12:2) Trust in the Lord with all your heart, And do not lean on your own understanding. In all your ways acknowledge Him, and He will make your paths straight. Do not be wise in your own eyes; Fear the Lord and turn away from evil. (Proverbs 3:5-7) ❊ "For My thoughts are not your thoughts, nor are your ways My ways," declares the Lord. "For as the heavens are higher than the earth, so are My ways higher than your ways and My thoughts than your thoughts." (Isaiah 55:8-9)

Living It Out

Think about the plans that God may have for your life and ministry. Are you ready and willing to follow God's lead or are you staying in the background, looking for a substitute to take your place? Make a point to do at least one thing this week that will bring you closer to fulfilling God's perfect plan for the gifts He's given you to bless others.

Drawing From the Well of Prayer

Lord, I submit my life to You, a living sacrifice. I choose to have my mind renewed, to be transformed from the world's way of thinking so that I might understand Your perfect will for my life. Lead me by Your Holy Spirit. Fill me with the knowledge of Your plan and give me strength and wisdom to make choices that will prepare and equip me for Your call.

Carol
Kent

Carol is a popular speaker
and writer. She has been
mentoring speakers for over
fifteen years through her
Speak Up With Confidence
seminars. Her books include:
*Becoming a Woman of
Influence, Tame Your Fears,
Mothers Have Angel Wings,
Speak Up With Confidence
and Secret Longings of
the Heart.*

GOD'S VISION– YOUR MISSION

As I was finishing another year as a Bible Study Fellowship leader, God's Spirit was stirring within me. I was sensing a "creative restlessness." I would look over the large audience of women each week representing a variety of backgrounds and I realized how many of them had a powerful story to tell. But they didn't know how to put their testimony together.

As I prayed about the restlessness I was feeling, God reminded me that my degrees were in speech education and in communication arts. After years of teaching speech and God's Word, perhaps I could equip people with communication skills that would further the kingdom of God.

Within six months I developed training materials and launched the communications training seminar that is now called

"Speak Up With Confidence." It started with fifteen women in my living room who were learning how to share their spiritual journeys in spoken form for the first time, and now the seminar is presented to thousands of men and women in cities across the United States and Canada.

It was Henrietta Mears who said, "There is no magic in small plans. When I consider my ministry, I think of the world. Anything less than that would not be worthy of Christ nor of His will for my life … What you *are* is God's gift to you. What you can *become* is your gift to Him."

What happens when you catch a vision of what God might be doing in your life and then you act on that dream?

You experience *risk*. When I left my job as the teaching leader for Bible Study Fellowship, I felt like I was risking giving up my sense of spiritual fulfillment.

You experience *fear*. The enemy approached me with hundreds of reasons why I could never be qualified to teach this group of women how to speak. For a while I wondered if launching this seminar was just an ego trip that would wind up making me feel like an idiot.

You experience *total dependence on God*. When you start feeling weak, you start seeking His face through prayer and Bible study.

You experience *joy*. There can be no greater joy than to "live in the smile of God's approval." I call it the eureka of knowing you are in God's will.

You receive *more assignments*. As God confirms your vision, new doors open. Current tasks are delegated to people who are ready to risk saying "yes" to Him. And "creative restlessness" returns. But this time, you know it's the Holy Spirit saying, "Listen up! I have another demanding but fulfilling task for you to do."

Author and speaker Jan Johnson writes, "When pondering dreams, many conclude: I could never do this … I'm not clever enough … it'll never succeed … But failure is normal, even essential. It is the fertile ground from which success arises. The question is not whether you've made some mistakes or failed in the past but whether you'll let fear keep you from trying."

Let's not let fear hold us back. Let's be more like Jesus. And let's start by embracing the vision He is birthing in our hearts.

Words of Life

Then the Lord answered me and said, "Record the vision and inscribe it on tablets, that the one who reads it may run. (Habakkuk 2:2) ❁ The mind of man plans his way, but the Lord directs his steps. (Proverbs 16:9) ❁ "For I know the plans I have for you," declares the Lord, "plans for welfare and not for calamity to give you a future and a hope." (Jeremiah 29:11)

Living It Out

Ask yourself what your passion is and what you would most love to do for your Heavenly Father and for others. Within your passion lies your mission. Start small, do something with the resources you have today. Seldom does a big vision start out big. Pray and seek the counsel and guidance of the Holy Spirit and follow His leadership in bringing about the vision He has birthed in your heart.

Drawing From the Well of Prayer

Father, help me to pay attention to "creative restlessness" that comes from You. Thank You for placing dreams within my heart that will lead me to living out Your vision for my life. Give me the courage to face my fears and realize those dreams.

CeCe
Winans

CeCe released her first solo
effort in 1995. She is an
eight-time Grammy Award
winner as a duo and solo act
and a nine-time Dove Award
winner. She has also earned
three NAACP Awards.

PRAY AND SING
FOR A VICTORY

I have seven brothers and two sisters, and each one of my siblings
is very special to me. I can't imagine life without any of them.
The experience of almost losing my brother Ronald changed
me forever.

My brother Marvin had driven Ronald to the hospital
because he had been complaining of a shortness of breath and
was coughing. The doctors discovered that Ronald had had a
major heart attack months before and didn't know it. After a
heart specialist examined Ronald, Marvin was advised to phone
the whole family.

We all flew in. My brother's life was hanging in the
balance. I will never forget the look on the doctors' faces when
after consulting among themselves they turned to the family

and informed us that there was nothing they could do to save my brother.

The family began to pray and we called everyone we knew and asked them to pray. We sang and we prayed. I could taste the fear creeping into my throat. My mouth grew dry when I saw Mom. How many times had I been comforted by her words, "The Lord will make a way somehow." Now she stood crying at the bedside of her second-oldest son. She was lost in her world of private memories.

We prayed and sang in Ronald's hospital room. We were singing for the life of one of our own. The next day the doctor modified his earlier prognosis and said that perhaps Ronald had a fifty-fifty chance if his aorta could be repaired.

We took shifts throughout the night before the operation. We sang over Ronald, anointed him with oil, prayed around his bed, and spoke words of encouragement into his ear. For a time it felt like warfare. We refused to entertain the thought of death. We were fighting for my brother's life with the only thing that we knew worked: prayer and pleading the blood of Jesus over him.

The next day as we waited for the results of the surgery, one of the doctors came down the corridor to meet with us. The expression on his face was grave. Ronald's heart had exploded on the operating table, he informed us. "We've done all we can do; it's between God and Ronald. I'm going back to try again. He's been dead approximately four minutes."

This time the family knelt wherever we could find a cleared space and turned our faces toward Jesus, begging for a miracle. We stayed like that for what seemed like hours. Finally, my cousin Dwayne came running down the hall screaming, "Nothing but good news! Ronald is going to recovery. Ronald is fine." Bedlam broke out in the halls of the hospital. "Praise the Lord!" "Thank You, Jesus!" we shouted. The tears flowed down my face as I watched Mom and Dad collapse in each other's arms.

A couple of the doctors confided that they felt the presence of the divine in the room as they operated. What makes Ronald's miracle all the more special is that it was borne on the wings of prayer—not only of his family, but also of people from across the country, friends and coworkers, hospital personnel, strangers in corridors—a platoon of mercy angels joining us in prayer.

Words of Life

And call upon Me in the day of trouble; I shall rescue you, and you will honor me. (Psalm 50:15) Truly I say to you, whoever says to this mountain, "Be taken up and cast into the sea," and does not doubt in his heart, but believes that what he says is going to happen, it will be granted him. (Mark 11:23) Additional Reading: Psalm 91

Living It Out

If you are facing a seemingly immovable mountain, ask the Lord to give you grace to persevere through the test. Pray and believe God's Word—that He is able to move mountains. God is bigger than symptoms, circumstances and evidence that is contrary to His promises.

Drawing From the Well of Prayer

Father God, thank You that I can count on You to be the Redeemer— not only of my soul, but of my circumstances. Give me wisdom to know when to hold on tight to Your Word and ask for a miracle in the face of immovable mountains in my life.

Anita Bryant

Anita is a well-known vocalist, an author and a speaker. As 1977 began she was known as the spokesperson for Florida orange juice, "The Sunshine Girl." Anita tells how God restored her to emotional health following her involvement in the political campaign that destroyed her marriage and career.

TAKING THE FIRST STEP TOWARD FORGIVENESS

In 1977, my world caved in. With a successful, high-profile career as an entertainer/author/songwriter, I was also a mom concerned about the education of my four children in Dade County, Florida. I led a referendum opposing legislation which would have required that homosexuals be hired as teachers in private religious schools. My stand quickly became national news. I lost contracts, bookings and, finally, my marriage of twenty years. I was caught between those who opposed my stand and those who condemned me for divorce.

Soon after my divorce, exhausted and anxious, with no husband, no job and no home, I felt I had nowhere to go. A dear friend, Bobbie Ames, welcomed me into her home.

"Bob's acting like a madman," I told her, referring to my

former husband's protests regarding our four children living with me instead of him. "I don't know where to go from here."

Bobbie interrupted me. Gently but authoritatively, she dropped her bombshell. "You go to your knees. We're going to ask God to forgive you for your sins against Bob and ask Him to help you forgive Bob for his sins and for everything he ever did to hurt you."

I felt trapped. Yet I listened as Bobbie continued. "You need to build a workable relationship with Bob, for your children. God expects you to be willing to try, Anita. The rest will follow."

Bobbie took my hands in hers, then asked God to lead me. Quivering, I confessed my openness to be willing to forgive. At last I raised my face, now wet with tears, and released a deep sigh. For the first time in months, I felt peace steal into my spirit. At that moment I realized that something new was about to happen. The road was making a U-turn, and I was headed toward healing. There would be miles and miles to go, but I had taken the first step.

When God guided me toward a righteous friend that day, I believe He saved me months, perhaps years, of anguish. That didn't mean the debris of the past wouldn't be brought up time after time. But once I had been to the foot of the Cross, at least I now recognized where to leave my unforgiveness.

Choosing to stay in unforgiveness makes us voluntary victims who stay emotionally stuck in the same old grooves; the needle plays our worn-out complaints again and again, while life passes us by.

Maybe you could use a little tough love in your life right now—the kind that Bobbie Ames gave me. Even if you're not used to praying or never before have approached God, you can do it now. He is here. When you confess your sins and then ask Him to help you forgive anyone who has sinned against you, a miracle will happen. God will help you take that first step.

Words of Life

And forgive us our debts, as we also have forgiven our debtors. For if you forgive men for their transgressions, your heavenly Father will also forgive you. But if you do not forgive others, then your Father will not forgive your transgressions. (Matthew 6:12, 14-15) 🌸 Therefore I say to you, all things for which you pray and ask, believe that you have received them, and they shall be granted you. Whenever you stand praying, forgive, if you have anything against anyone, so that your Father who is in heaven will forgive you your transgressions. (Mark 11:24-25) 🌸 Do not judge and you will not be judged; and do not condemn, and you will not be condemned; pardon, and you will be pardoned. (Luke 6:37)

Living It Out

If the heaviness of unforgiveness is weighing you down and keeping you from rising to peace and joy in your life, take a moment to write down the name or names of people you need to forgive.

Ask God to help you forgive, and then say aloud, "God, I forgive _____ (the person who hurt you) for _____ (name the hurtful situation)." Remember that forgiveness is a process and that you have taken the first important step. Trust God to complete the process in His perfect time.

If you feel that you may need to get in touch with the person you need to forgive, consider discussing your thoughts with a wise friend or trained counselor first.

Drawing From the Well of Prayer

Dear God, I want to forgive. I want to live in the fullness of Your peace and joy. Please take hold of my hand and lead me as I take the first steps toward forgiving those who have hurt me.

Anna Kendall

Anna is an ordained minister, author, speaker and lecturer. She is the vice president and co-founder of the Family Restoration Network and the Life Languages Institute, Dallas, Texas. She has served as host of a weekly television program and numerous radio talk shows. She and her husband, Fred, reside in the Dallas area.

WHEN IT STORMS... FORECAST FAITH!

A few years back, a terrible storm barreled into our city of Dallas, Texas. My husband, Fred, was at a speaking engagement, and I was at home with our son, Michael, who was visiting from college on spring break. As we watched the churning, inky skies from our patio door, a sudden flash of lightning revealed a deadly tornado whirling straight toward our home.

The next few moments seemed to move in slow motion. Michael yelled, "Run to the bathtub!" I gathered up our two shelties and hurried into the bathroom, but quickly noticed that Michael was missing. I then saw him pulling his mattress down the hall to protect us, but it got stuck in the doorway. Abandoning the mattress, he and I jumped into the bathtub with the two dogs.

Seconds later the storm hit full force, creating unnerving music as the pipes in the house wheezed and hummed. Our quartet in the bathtub chimed right in: Michael loudly quoted Psalm 91, I commanded the storm to be still in the name of Jesus, and both dogs alternated between barking and howling. We were accompanied by the splintering, crashing noises of our roof being ripped off. Electrical lines were yanked loose, sending the house and our frantic crew into uncertain blackness.

The departing tornado was followed by an eerie calm and complete silence. Providentially, we were not hurt and our house was the least damaged on our block.

Fred came home, and with the help of neighbors and firemen, constructed a temporary cover on our roof, but the rains continued. By the next night the ceiling in the master bedroom had absorbed so much water that it collapsed onto our bed at three o'clock in the morning. Michael ran into our room and found us in the middle of the bed covered with black, wet globs of insulation.

I slowly stood up through the layers of mushy debris. My wet hair was plastered against my face and my hands were set defiantly on my hips. It was decision time. I was either going to become hysterical, or I had to make a faith declaration. (Later my husband said that my delivery was reminiscent of Scarlet in *Gone With the Wind*.) Through tears I resolved, "I don't care what happens, we're not going to let this tornado steal our joy or rob us of our faith. We're going to praise the Lord in all things!"

With that dramatic proclamation, we all three fell into a heap on the slippery floor and broke into gales of laughter. Looking around our storm-struck home, we talked about what was truly precious and valuable in life and what was not. As we went down the list, we realized we had so much to be thankful for—especially that no one was hurt and we were all together.

When unexpected and unwanted circumstances catch you off guard, it's easy to lose heart and buckle under the mounting pressure. It's okay to be honest with God and express your feelings. At some point though, it is often necessary to make a choice, even a declaration, that you will choose faith over fear and joy over discontent. May you too discover what our family did on that crazy, stormy night: that thanksgiving mixed with joy and laughter can bring peace in the midst of life's storms.

Words of Life

The joy of the Lord is your strength. (Nehemiah 8:10) 🌸 Giving thanks for all things in the name of our Lord Jesus Christ to God the Father. (Ephesians 5:20) 🌸 Extract the precious from the worthless. (Jeremiah 15:19)

Living It Out

Are you focusing on what you don't have or your bad breaks, rather than looking at what you do have? Take a good look at what is really valuable in life and thank God for His blessings. Our greatest blessing is Jesus—because of Him we don't have to handle life's problems and challenges alone.

Drawing From the Well of Prayer

Father, please forgive me for the times I have complained and murmured, rather than praised and trusted You. Open my eyes to separate the precious things in my life from what is of no eternal value. When I'm faced with the storms of life, help me to know that You are big enough to handle my smallest needs.

PART TWO: SOUL

Betty Robison

Betty co-hosts the LIFE TODAY show with her husband, James Robison. She is the mother of three children and the grand- mother of eleven. She has been married for over thirty- eight years and resides in the Dallas-Fort Worth area.

WAITING FOR GOD'S BEST

Our first child, Rhonda, was three years old when I had an ovary removed. The doctor said that I had endometriosis and advised me to focus on enjoying my daughter because I would probably not be able to conceive any more children. My heart sank. I longed to have a son. I cried out to God with the prayer of Hannah in the first chapter of 1 Samuel, "Oh Lord Almighty, if only You will look down upon my sorrow and answer my prayer and give me a son!" When my miracle didn't come, I grew jealous of other women around me who were able to have babies, and worse yet, I became bitter and angry at God.

One day in my brokenness over this spiritual impasse, I finally released my hurt and anger to God. I asked Him to heal me of the profound disappointment of not being able to have another child. I asked him to fill the empty space inside me. I told Him with tears streaming down my face, "I just want to live for You. I want to relish every moment You've given me to spend with my precious Rhonda."

In time, God graciously began to take away the yearning I had to give birth to a son. And, amazingly, He filled my heart with a peace and contentment that I had previously thought was impossible. With the contentment, there came a peaceful desire to check into adoption. James and I applied with several agencies with the help of a lawyer friend. After our first meeting with him, he started the paperwork and the wait began. Providentially, exactly nine months from the date of that meeting, our son Randy came into the world and into our hearts forever.

The first time James and I saw Randy, our eyes filled with tears of pure joy. We loved him from that first moment and have never stopped since! There was no difference in the intensity of our love for our adopted son and the love for our biological daughter.

Over three years later, I began to feel unusually tired and a little queasy. I was concerned that maybe the endometriosis was back in full force. I went to the doctor thinking I had cancer. Instead, James and I found out that a miracle was in full force—I was pregnant! And on November 18, 1972, Robin Rochelle Robison, our miracle baby, joined our family, making it complete.

As I tucked my three little R's into bed one night and gave them a good-night kiss, I reflected on God's perfect plan. He had wanted me to have His best. If He had given me what

I wanted, when I wanted it, I would have never known our wonderful son, Randy.

Since then, whenever my heart is hurting over a troubling situation, I strive to remember that God has a plan and He sees the whole picture. He knows *what* I need and *when* I need it. Although it can be hard to wait on God, I cling to the truth that God wants to bless me with *His* best, in *His* perfect time.

Words of Life

For the Lord God is a sun and shield; The Lord gives grace and glory; No good thing does He withhold from those who walk uprightly. O Lord of hosts, How blessed is the man who trusts in You! (Psalm 84:11-12) ✻ He makes the barren woman abide in the house as a joyful mother of children. Praise the Lord! (Psalm 113:9) ✻ So there remains a Sabbath rest for the people of God. For the one who has entered His rest has himself also rested from his works, as God did from His. Therefore let us be diligent to enter that rest, so that no one will fall through following the same example of disobedience. (Hebrews 4:9-11) ✻ For I am confident of this very thing, that He who began a good work in you will perfect it until the day of Christ Jesus. For it is God who is at work in you, both to will and to work for His good pleasure. (Philippians 1:6; 2:13)

Living It Out

Ephesians 2:10 says that we were created for good works—the kind that are done through dependence on God. Remember that the work being done in your life is God's work. Therefore, it will be done on His timetable. Rest in God's ability and reap the supernatural results. Be careful not to rob yourself of joy, peace and fulfillment while He is working, by fretting over the time He is taking to get it done. Remember that God demonstrates His heart of sensitivity toward us by blessing us with His best, in His time.

Drawing From the Well of Prayer

My soul glorifies and magnifies You, Lord, and my spirit rejoices in You, my Savior! For You have been mindful of the humble state of Your servant . . . You have done great things for me. Holy is Your name. (Luke 1:46-55)—*The prayer of Mary, mother of Jesus as she realized that she indeed was pregnant with the Christ Child.*

Becky Tirabassi

Becky is a highly regarded motivational and inspirational speaker and author, as well as founder and president of Change Your Life, Inc. She has produced fitness videos and has also written a number of books including, *Let Faith Change Your Life*, and *Wild Things Happen When I Pray*. Her newest book is *Change Your Life*.

RESTORING RELATIONSHIPS

It began when I was a teenager. My mom and I have always had a very robust style of interaction. We developed a loud, demeaning and hostile pattern of communication. By the time I turned twenty-one, married and had a child, my relationship with my mother became less hostile, but I did not want to spend time with her. She was happy about my sobriety, spirituality and maturity, but our core personalities still clashed.

When I became an author and began to make public speaking appearances, I spoke freely about my volatile teen-age years. In 1994, I returned home to Cleveland to share my story in front of forty thousand people. My entire extended family and numerous friends were planning to come. Just before I got in the car to drive downtown, my mother took me aside. Through tears, she shared that she was afraid that I was going to humiliate her and my father with the details of our family's past. Though I thought I had been helping others with my story, in the process I had been exposing and wounding my mother and father every time I spoke!

I promised my mother that from that day on I would not describe our relationship and family life in the way in which I had been freely exposing and condemning them for years. I told her I would only give the details about my past, rather than exploit my parents' lives in public. As months and years went by, I kept my word, but I still did not want to spend any length of time with my parents. (This should have been a red flag to alert me of my unforgivingness). I held my parents at arm's length, emotionally—not exhibiting a warm, childlike affection when I was with them.

One night I attended a small group meeting where women shared deep pain from their past. But rather than wallow in self-pity, we were encouraged to apologize in writing to someone we had hurt. I reflected back to the incident in 1994. Further journaling revealed how I had never sincerely asked my parents to forgive me for how I had hurt them. I wrote a letter to my mother telling her how sorry I was for wanting to hurt her and for publicly humiliating her in my speeches and books. I told her I loved her and I wanted to have a loving relationship with her. I humbly asked her to forgive me. However, by the end of the week, I threw the letter away, thinking it had served the purpose of revealing my unwillingness to heal my relationship with my mother.

On Saturday, I called my mother. She asked, "Why did you call, Becky?"

I replied, "I don't know."

She said, "You won't believe this. I was just listening to an old tape of your story. It is one of the times when you shared how terrible we were as parents. It made me cry."

"I do know why I called," I whispered quietly.

Then I apologized in depth for trying to hurt her, for being unforgiving, and for exposing so much of her life to other people without her permission. I asked her to forgive me.

She said, "Becky, I've always felt terrible about how unhappy your teen-age years were. Your dad and I were struggling to survive financially, and in other ways. I am ashamed for how dad and I hurt you when you were a child. I never wanted my friends to think that our lives were so out of control. I am so sorry for the pain I have caused you. Will you forgive me?"

I was speechless, I had waited twenty-two years to hear my mother say those words. I had tried to manipulate and orchestrate ways to get her to apologize to me, validating my pain. But those words never came. I replied, "It's a miracle!"

Immediately, a favorite verse came to mind, "Confess your sins to one another so that you may be healed." My confession and admission resulted not only in my mother's healed emotions, but I was touched and healed when she asked me to forgive her.

Words of Life

For if you forgive men for their transgressions, your heavenly Father will also forgive you. But if you do not forgive others, then your Father will not forgive your

transgressions. (Matthew 6:14-15) ✖ Bearing with one another,

and forgiving each other, whoever has a complaint against anyone;

just as the Lord forgave you, so also should you. (Colossians 3:13)

✖ Heal me, O Lord, and I will be healed; Save me and I will be

saved, for You are my praise. (Jeremiah 17:14)

Living It Out

You can begin to heal your emotions and relationships by reaching

into your soul to discover when you have been hurt. Ask yourself

what *kinds* of situations tend to hurt you, and most importantly,

why they hurt.

Asking and answering honest questions is the first step

in developing an awareness that can lead to inner healing. Write

your thoughts, conflicts, fears and unresolved issues down. Pray

about them and follow the leadership of the Holy Spirit in asking

for forgiveness and bringing restorations to your relationships. If

necessary, seek the aide of a professional or lay counselor.

Drawing From the Well of Prayer

Father God, thank You that You want to set me free from painful memories and circumstances that keep me from being all that I can be in You. Give me wisdom, sensitivity and strength to deal appropriately and decisively with the emotional baggage that weighs me down. Let me rest in knowing deep within that when my burdens are heavy, Your yoke is light.

Sheila Walsh

Sheila is one of the keynote speakers for the popular *Women of Faith* conferences. She is known for her work on the *700 Club*, the Family Channel's *Heart to Heart* daily talk show and the BBC's *The Rock Gospel* show. As a singer and songwriter she has been nominated for Dove and Grammy Awards. She is also the author of fourteen books.

FACE
YOUR FEARS

At the peak of my career as co-host of the 700 Club, my life crumbled around me. I was pushing myself punishingly hard, keeping an impossible schedule of concerts. I realized that I was feeling empty, detached, angry and very sad inside. My condition progressively got worse, until, one day in October 1992, I admitted myself to a Christian psychiatric hospital.

Upon my admission, everything was taken away from me … my belongings, toiletries, etc. I lay on the floor, weeping. That is when I discovered that Christ lives very close to the floor. During my treatment, I wrote this poem:

> *I never knew you lived so close to the floor,*
> *but every time I am bowed down,*
> *crushed by this weight of grief,*

I feel your hand on my head,

your breath on my cheek,

your tears on my neck

You never tell me to pull myself together,

to stem the flow of many years.

You simply stay by my side

for as long as it takes,

so close to the floor.

Due in part to losing my father to brain disease when I was a young girl, fear, anger, need for approval, and loneliness were deeply rooted in me. When a doctor asked me what I was so afraid of, I answered, "I'm afraid if the fancy wrapping of my life were taken away, and I looked inside the box, it would be empty."

Until this crisis I had never known what an awesome companion the Lord longs to be. I had spent so many years trying to make Him proud of me, determined to never fail, that I missed the most amazing gift of all: to be able "to bury my face in the mane of the Lion of Judah," as Stuart Henderson so eloquently wrote.

During treatment I found that God is indeed a mighty lion. And when I am in trouble, I can either hide my face from Him or run to Him and let Him hide me in His mane. There I will find strength to live my life.

Courage is developed by embracing our greatest fears and not being deterred by them. I had to begin with the woman that I was and, by pressing on, find courage to become the woman I wanted to be.

I decided to start listening to what God had to say about my life. It was not easy, but I knew that it would give me courage to be real with other people, to be vulnerable, and to stop seeking security and strength in the approval of others.

One of the greatest gifts God would give us is peace of mind. The demands of our lives constantly pester us. But even though life is difficult and demanding, the perfect love of Jesus has the power to drive out even our most devastating fears. So go ahead, run to Him and bury your head in His mighty mane.

Words of Life

I sought the Lord, and He answered me, and delivered me from all my fears. (Psalm 34:4)
There is no fear in love, but perfect love casts out fear. (1 John 4:18a) The Lord is my light and my salvation; Whom shall I fear? The Lord is the defense of my life; Whom shall I dread? (Psalm 27:1)

Living It Out

A great way to start facing your fears is to name them. Write down your fears and then look at them in light of Scripture. There are so many Scriptures that encourage us or even *command* us, "Do not be afraid." And finally, the book of Psalms can be a particularly powerful tool as you pray them out loud to battle your fears.

Drawing From the Well of Prayer

Dear God, please give me the courage to face the fears that hold me back from becoming the woman I want to be.

Valorie Burton

Valorie is president of The Burton Agency, a marketing and public relations firm in Dallas, Texas. She is a former Miss Black Texas USA and a runner-up to Miss Texas. She is a frequent columnist and speaker.

DON'T DOWNSIZE YOUR DREAM

My parents always encouraged me to "dream big" and supported me in pursuing my dreams. I have learned that every single thing I do is a choice—even doing nothing is a choice. Living my life with purpose and passion is one of the best choices I ever made.

I find that many women don't live the lives they want to live or do the things they want to do. Most don't realize that they have a lot more control over their lives than they believe they do. Why are so few of us doing what we love?

Each of us has a passion for *something*. What is that "something" in your life that would make you jump out of bed in the morning, excited about the day ahead? If you have determined your most desired goal, yet you find yourself pursuing it indirectly, then you have allowed fear to downsize your dream. Instead of fearlessly pursuing the goal, you have settled for doing something that perhaps draws on similar skills and is easier to pursue.

For example, the world is filled with English teachers who have dreamed of writing novels, but never took that first step. Instead, they work in a profession that requires them to teach about novels, read novels and teach students the basics of writing. Yet they have never used those skills to fulfill a lifelong dream of being a novelist.

I have found that creating a personal mission statement helps to create a gauge by which you can assess everything you choose to do in life. It is a single sentence that is broad enough to encompass your work and personal life and narrow enough to define the underlying purpose in all you do. To write a mission statement, you must listen to the innermost part of your being. What does your inner voice tell you it needs for complete fulfillment? Your inner voice is often God's way of speaking to you, and you should listen carefully.

Your mission statement will give clarity to your life. Decisions will become easier to make, and bad situations will become more obvious. You will feel a pressing need to either fix those bad situations or let them go altogether.

Once you have a mission statement, it can be translated into a God-inspired vision. A vision is what drives you as you carry out your mission. Your vision is the "ideal" of where you want to be. Your mission explains *how* you should do what you do and your vision explains *why.*

Finally, it is crucial to set goals that are consistent with your mission and vision. One of the many lessons I have learned in business is that there is power in the written word. You can move your goals from dream to reality by writing them down.

Pursue your goals vigorously and don't let fear step in and downsize your dream. In time, you will find yourself living the life you want to live—a life of fulfillment, passion and purpose.

Words of Life

For God hath not given us the spirit of fear; but of power, and of love, and of a sound mind. (2 Timothy 1:7 KJV) ✼ Where there is no vision, the people perish. (Proverbs 29:18a KJV) ✼ Brethren, I do not regard myself as having laid hold of it yet; but one thing I do: forgetting what lies behind and reaching forward to what lies ahead, I press on toward the goal for the prize of the upward call of God in Christ Jesus. (Philippians 3:13-14)

Living It Out

Ask God to guide you as you write out a personal mission statement for your life, vocation or a specific role you play in life (wife, mother, employee, etc.). Then begin to create a vision statement based upon that God-given mission. Finally, write down specific, measurable goals that will lead to the fulfillment of your vision. Start a "goal journal" in order to elaborate on your goals and jot down ideas as they come to you.

Drawing From the Well of Prayer

Father, infuse my heart with a sense of high purpose. Help me discover what it is that You created me to do. Give me the motivation and perseverance to fulfill that God-given mission.

Rebecca St. James

Rebecca has been singing since she was sixteen years old. Rebecca moved to the United States with her whole family from Australia in 1991. Her family's commitment to her success paid off when in 1994 she signed with Forefront Records. Rebecca, who does two hundred concerts a year, won a Grammy for her fourth album, *Pray*.

FEED YOUR MIND

I love to read. In my bag that travels with me everywhere, I always carry two translations of the Bible, my diary and usually a Christian book. I especially love Christian historical fiction because I believe we can learn a lot from the past.

We are so fortunate to be able to read and to fill our minds with things that are going to grow us in our relationship with God and help us in our lives. Our minds are really like the most incredible computer your can imagine! Our minds remember everything. Consequently, we need to be very careful to fill our heads with things that are pure. We need to be set apart for God— to be used by Him.

It may be that sometimes we just need to say to God, "Lord, purify my mind. Help me to start over today and resist the temptation to fill my mind with things that are not of You. Give me a distaste for evil, and more and more of a love and a desire for You." I love the prayer that says, "Create in me a pure heart, O God, and renew a steadfast spirit within me." (Psalm 51:10 NIV)

Most of us women love to eat. Maybe that's the reason God uses a culinary analogy when discussing the true soul food:

"Don't waste your energy striving for perishable food like that. Work for the food that sticks with you, food that nourishes your lasting life, food the Son of Man provides. He and what he does are guaranteed by God the Father to last." (John 6:26, The Message)

As you live this week with the Lord, be aware of what you are feeding your mind, and remember that what you feed your mind affects the condition of your soul.

Words of Life

The mind of the intelligent seeks knowledge, but the mouth of fools feeds on folly. (Proverbs 15:14) ❧ So, every good tree bears good fruit, but the bad tree bears bad fruit. A good tree cannot produce bad fruit, nor can a bad tree produce good fruit. Every tree that does not bear good fruit is cut down and thrown into the fire. So then, you will know them by their fruits. (Matthew 7:17-20) ❧ In reference to your former manner of life, you lay aside the old self, which is being corrupted in accordance with the lusts of deceit, and that you be renewed in the spirit of your mind, and put on the new self, which in the likeness of God has been created in righteousness and holiness of the truth. (Ephesians 4:22-24)

Living It Out

Compare your spiritual growth to eating by looking over this

checklist. Ask yourself:

Do I tend to

1. Try to survive on one meal a week?

2. Eat two to three meals a day?

3. Fast so long that I should not be alive?

4. Exist on junk food?

5. Live on bread and water?

6. Eat regularly?

Then ask yourself:

1. To really feed my mind on things that honor God,

what do I need to do less of?

2. What kind of "junk food" is clogging my spiritual brain cells?

3. Besides the Bible, what else should I be feeding my mind?

Drawing From the Well of Prayer

Lord God, with Your help, I want to feed my mind and my soul with things that will inspire me to shine for You. In reaching for that goal, I plan to make the following changes in my spiritual diet: (List changes that you want to make on a sheet of paper or your prayer journal.)

Martha Williamson

Martha is the award-winning executive producer and head writer for the inspirational television series *Touched by an Angel.* In addition to her twenty-year career in television, drama, comedy and variety, she is also a popular speaker and author. Martha is married to Jon Andersen, co-executive producer of *Touched by an Angel.*

SOMETHING OLD ... SOMETHING NEW

As a Christian who writes a television show about God, I am in the unique position of putting words in His mouth every week. I do my best to represent God as biblically and accurately as possible on a network TV series. It is an awesome responsibility, especially since I am attempting to set forth ideal standards that I value but don't always live up to myself. I don't know anyone who can do that without the grace and mercy of God. Nevertheless, in my experience—especially in my failures—I have found years' worth of stories to tell and lessons to share.

One of the greatest lessons I have ever learned has yet to become an episode of *Touched by an Angel.* It was during the months of my engagement to my wonderful husband Jon.

When I was preparing for my wedding, I had an inherent

need to have brand-new everything: brand-new shoes, a brand-new dress, even brand-new underwear. This is a common instinct as a bride. Usually the only things that aren't new are your sentimental items: your grandmother's pearls, your best friend's bracelet or your mother's veil.

In the same way, there is often the desire to walk down the aisle with a new heart and a purified soul. Only here, you can't afford to hold onto anything old for sentimental reasons. You will have a need in your heart and your mind to come clean in every way that you can.

I was considered by my high-school friends to be "square." I went to church on Sundays; I didn't "go all the way." I thought I would be a virgin until my wedding night. But it didn't happen that way, and I didn't get married until I was forty-two. I never lived with anyone. But there were lonely times, too. And like many women I know, I was willing to trade all sorts of things, including my values to ease that loneliness. Needless to say, I only ended up lonelier.

I don't think I fully realized the destructive power of some of my behavior until Jon and I seriously began to consider marriage. But sooner or later, it all catches up with you, and when that happens, that is a terrible day. Nevertheless, through God's abundant grace, I realized there was, in fact, a way to truly become new again and approach the wedding altar with the sense of a fresh beginning that I had imagined as a girl. The process began with the discovery of "soul ties."

Soul ties are the strong emotional and spiritual attachments that you create with other people. Someone once described it this way: When you get involved with someone—and certainly when you are intimate with someone—it's like gluing two pieces of wood together. Then, when you finally pull the wood apart, it doesn't come off clean. Each takes a little piece of the other away with it.

So, how do you go about getting rid of all those glued-on pieces of other people? How do you get to the point where a man from your past has no pull anymore?

The answer came for Jon and I during a retreat called the "Cleansing Stream." Along with many others, we were invited to write a list of all our past relationships, both physical and emotional. As I wrote, I could feel how much I wanted back all those pieces of myself that I had left glued to other people. And how much I wanted to be rid of the pieces that were still glued to me.

In prayer we brought each name on our lists before the Lord. We asked God to forgive us, and we committed ourselves to turn away from our past relationships and past behaviors. One by one, we crossed the names off. Finally, we ripped up our lists and said goodbye to our past forever, acknowledging that it no longer had any power over us.

Suddenly I felt healed and whole again, free of the pieces of other people that I had been carrying around. And all the pieces of myself that I had given away were gathered and returned to me. I hadn't felt like that in years. I felt cleansed and I was ready to marry Jon. He was now truly my one and only. And I was truly his.

Words of Life

Therefore if anyone is in Christ, he is a new creature; the old things

passed away; behold, new things have come. (2 Corinthians 5:17)

 Brethren, I do not regard myself as having laid hold of it yet;

but one thing I do: forgetting what lies behind and reaching forward

to what lies ahead ... (Philippians 3:13)

Drawing From the Well of Prayer

Write your own

prayer here.

Robin Turner

Robin Turner, the younger daughter of James and Betty Robison, is married to Ken Turner. The couple live in Tulsa, Oklahoma, with their children. She devotes herself full-time to her ministry as a wife and mother.

THE BEST JOB
IN THE WORLD

When I was a young girl, people would ask me what I wanted to be when I grew up. From the time I can remember I would tell them I wanted to be a wife and mother. I even dressed up as a homemaker for career day in the ninth grade. I chose this as my career and I think it is the most rewarding job there is.

But in spite of my strong maternal instincts, there are still days when I feel like I'm fighting a losing battle when it comes to training my children. Despite numerous, sometimes valiant efforts to correct undesirable behavior in my irresistible offspring, I find myself transformed into a parental Rocky—back in the ring, going the distance with a recurring problem.

Then something will happen to remind me that maybe all my effort and prayers are not in vain, after all. For example, one day when my children were small, I became very frustrated with them and was growing more impatient by the moment. One of the boys dripped his juice in a trail up the stairs, when he knew to keep it in the kitchen. My bad attitude simply made theirs worse.

As I was putting folded laundry away, slamming the drawer shut and grumbling under my breath, Christopher looked at me with his big, blue eyes and said, "Mom, you're not rejoicing in the Lord always!" Well, did that ever wake me up! This was the same verse that I had often quoted to the children, and now it was coming back to me—from the mouth of my babe.

I got down on my knees and turned to Christopher and said, "You're right, son. Mommy needs to ask God's forgiveness, and I need to ask your forgiveness too." He wrapped his sweet, little arms around my neck, gave me a tight squeeze and said, "That's okay, Mommy. I forgive you." I then chose by an act of my will to change my attitude and be joyful. The result was that I had a much better day and my children became more joyful as well.

Later that day I realized that my young son had showed signs of spiritual sensitivity. This is something all Christian parents hope to instill in their children, and I felt blessed to be witnessing it in Christopher at such a young age. God spoke to me through my son and not only showed me what I needed to change, but also showed me that my children really are hearing what I'm teaching.

Even though motherhood doesn't pay a salary, it pays in ways that far exceed a paycheck. Whenever my children learn something new from tying their shoes to sharing a toy without a fight, to seeing their love for Jesus grow each day, it's like a promotion for me.

As with any job I have days I would love to sleep in or quit, but then my kids will do or say the sweetest thing to melt my heart and inspire me to get up and keep going. It's like God is my boss and He gives me unexpected bonuses through the hugs and hearts of my children. God gave me this job and He knows I can handle it and sends encouragement when I need it most.

Motherhood is about crumbs on the floor, spots on the mirror and leaving them, while you play a game with your children or create a pint-sized masterpiece with colored paper, scissors and glue. My children will not remember that I kept a perfect house, but I hope they will remember that I made a haven of our home—and that I loved my job.

Words of Life

Train up a child in the way he should go, even when he is old he will not depart from it. (Proverbs 22:6) Rejoice in the Lord always; again I will say, rejoice! (Philippians 4:4) A joyful heart makes a cheerful face, but when the heart is sad, the spirit is broken. (Proverbs 15:13)

Living It Out

If it sometimes seems that you are getting nowhere with your childrearing, don't give up. Keep the faith, choose to maintain a positive attitude and stay in the Word—it is our guide for every problem. Give your past failures to God. Keep your eyes focused on the future and believe that God will bless your faithfulness as you train your children for His glory.

Drawing From the Well of Prayer

Dear God, please give me the grace and wisdom to train my children in such a way that their hearts will want to honor You. Help me to hold onto Your Word as my guide in life and childrearing. Thank You for being a loving, encouraging "Boss" to this sometimes weary, but always grateful . . . mother.

Luci Swindoll

After an early retirement from a career with a major oil company, Luci became vice president of public relations at Insight For Living, her brother Chuck Swimdoll's international radio ministry. From there she "retired" to fulfill an ambitious speaking schedule, traveling across the United States, motivating and inspiring her audiences. She has written seven books and co-authored three.

CELEBRATING WORK

While working for several years as an executive at an oil company, I have found out that many people gravitate to one of two ways of looking at work. Many of us embrace the idea that work is an affliction, a drudgery, a crushing burden against society which deforms us and holds us back from being all we could be if we just didn't have to report to a job.

The opposite viewpoint is that work is not a curse, it is humanity's greatest blessing. Were it not for the virtue of work, all our idleness would be wasted or misspent in such a fashion that we would be in constant trouble or mischief.

My question is, "Why can't there be a happy medium?" Our job should be one where our labor produces dignity, self-respect, and an attitude of happy diligence. We need to stop looking at work as simply a means to earning a living and start realizing it is one of the elemental ingredients of making a life!

My friend and co-worker, Joe Hancock, had a gift for balancing hard work with relaxation on the job. He once told me, "Luci, we can view work as something handed down to us, thanks to Adam, and we are now forced to work. Or, work can be viewed as an extension of one's ministry. I believe when work has a place in our reason for being here, it keeps us balanced."

Joe often talked about Christians getting out of the salt shaker and into the workplace. He felt that Christians should "flavor the work environment" by being the people who add the spice—who add enjoyment to whatever we do.

One day when Joe and I were having lunch I asked him, "When you're retired, what would you like most to have said of you?" He leaned back in his chair and smiled mischievously as he cupped his chin with his hand, thinking carefully. He finally said, "I'd like people to say that they enjoyed working with me because I made work fun. I would consider it a very high compliment if people just said, 'Joe Hancock? Oh, yeah … I always enjoyed being around that guy.'"

Now that's "flavoring the work environment!" I like that phrase. It sums up the secret of celebrating work. I'm grateful for my friend Joe. His philosophies helped me see the hidden but essential ingredients of balancing our Monday through Fridays, our nine to fives. And when we find that balance, we will find ourselves able to truly celebrate the work and work environment that God has given us.

Words of Life

He also who is slack in his work is brother to him who destroys. (Proverbs 18:9) 🌿 The soul of the sluggard craves and gets nothing, but the soul of the diligent is made fat. (Proverbs 13:4) 🌿 Do you see a man skilled in his work? He will stand before kings; he will not stand before obscure men. (Proverbs 22:29)

Living It Out

Remind yourself that "Success is a journey, not a destination."

Happiness is to be found along the way, not at the end of the road,

for then the journey is over and it is too late. Today, this hour,

this minute, is the time for each of us to sense the fact that life is

good, with all its trials and troubles, and perhaps more interesting

because of them.

Drawing From the Well of Prayer

Dear Lord, give me

Your perspective on how

to integrate my work

and ministry rather than

compartmentalize them.

Open my eyes to the

wonder of Your presence

and guidance as I live each

moment of every day.

Ellie Kay

Ellie, who is known as the Coupon Queen, is a mother of five. Her sense of humor and system for saving money has made her a favorite speaker at ladies' retreats, Christian women's clubs and civic organizations. Her *Shop, Save and Share* seminars have been presented to audiences across the nation and even made into a film for the Air Force Family Aid Society.

SIMPLY SPEAKING: LET'S GET A GRIP!

The modern life gives us tons of options and opportunities that are often obstacles to the simple life. At the end of some days, I'm exhausted. And yet I feel as if I've only run the first leg of a 1,000-mile, 100-day race across the country. I know that every day this week will be just as action-paced, just as complex. I'm not alone. At one time or another, everyone feels, as the Air Force says, "overtasked and undermanned."

Well, there's good news for complex lives: there's hope for us. We can—simply speaking—get a grip!

I learned a lesson in simplifying the complex from observing my young daughter, Bethany. Ever since she was old enough to hold a crayon and find an empty wall, Bethany's been a writer. Sometimes she writes her feelings through pictures, but as her language skills progress, she writes her thoughts as poems. Here's a poem she wrote when she was six years old to a pair of sisters in our neighborhood.

No one is good as you two.

No one hass a Better Time,

You two.

And you two our the best ever.

Yes, I suppose I'm biased, but I think this little girl has talent. She writes, colors and pastes her way into the hearts of friends and family, neighbors and even acquaintances. Bethany has the uncanny ability to encourage people when the world beats them down and leaves them for lost. And she doesn't waste time or energy mincing words!

We can learn something from Bethany's knack for getting straight to the heart of a matter. Take our schedules, for instance. If we think about the beautiful things we want to enjoy and attain in life in the midst of an ugly, busy schedule, we too can bring simplicity out of complexity.

Why not write a list of the regular commitments, responsibilities, daily tasks and additional duties for the past two weeks? Don't forget the activities of your child and your spouse; they impact your life too. Also add up the hours spent in front of the television and on the computer.

You should have a substantial list! I sure did—I didn't even realize I was doing so much stuff until it was written down. When we look at our lives in black and white, we have to ask, "Why?"

Sometimes you may have to say *no* to the "pressing" things of life in order to pursue the "important" things in life. When we write these activities on paper, we can prioritize and evaluate the importance of the "stuff" that fills our schedules—and our lives.

Let's go one step further. When you look at your "A List" (activities list), what activities are unimportant and yet still on your list? Do you have time for the important or only the urgent? Why not pray about your schedule and ask the Father to help you order your life—to take the complex and make it a little simpler?

Once you develop a more manageable schedule and begin spending your time doing what's truly important to you, may you too, like Bethany, begin to focus on all that's right and beautiful about the people and world around you!

Words of Life

Cast your burden upon the Lord, and He will sustain you; He will never allow the righteous to be shaken. (Psalm 55:22) Do all things without grumbling or disputing; so that you will prove yourselves to be blameless and innocent, children of God above reproach in the midst of a crooked and perverse generation, among whom you appear as lights in the world. (Philippians 2:14-15)

And whatever we ask we receive from Him, because we keep His commandments and do the things that are pleasing in His sight. (1 John 3:22)

Living It Out

Write down your "A List" of responsibilities today and cross out the things that are not important. Focus your efforts and time, instead, on the things that are of true value to you and your family. You may find this difficult at first. However, with practice, you will get better at it. Eventually, you will realize that you are making your own choices about the use of your time instead of having the outside demands of life dictate how you live.

Drawing From the Well of Prayer

Help me, Lord, to slow down the pace of my life long enough to take inventory of how I am spending my time. Give me wisdom to make the best choices of how to spend each day and give me the discipline to say no to things that would keep me from pursuing what is really important to me and my family.

Terry
Dorian, Ph.D.

Terry has been a health researcher for over twenty years. She is considered an expert in the use of whole foods for the prevention and cure of degenerative disease. Dr. Dorian has authored several books and is a popular speaker and a radio and television personality.

REST IN STRESS: THE OVERCOMING LIFE

As children of God, we know that every circumstance in our lives has a purpose and a plan. God uses all of the happy and unhappy events in our lives to conform us to His image (Romans 8:29). But it takes time to learn this rock-bottom truth of our faith, and I did not know the truth of Romans 8:29 until my first husband died.

During that stressful time, my prayers became arguments with God. I could not, I would not, accept the circumstances. The finality of death tormented me. I could do nothing, absolutely nothing to alter the finality of death. However, I eventually submitted to His Word, and one day in May of 1978, not quite two months after Frank died, I read Romans chapter 8 as though for the first time. I saw the truth; I believed it; I realized that God loved Frank and God loved me! I would come to love His plan.

I have learned that confessing, repenting, and receiving God's grace and mercy are the basis of every victory we enjoy in Christ, and that is certainly true of victory over stress. The Word cleanses us as the Holy Spirit prepares our hearts.

The Lord Himself tells us in John 15:3 that we are clean because of the Word that He has spoken to us. The faith which brings forth our redemption comes into our hearts by the power of His Word. "So faith comes through hearing, and hearing by the word of Christ." (Romans 10:17)

Many stress management writers, even Christian ones, tell us to "manage stress" by making sure that we have proper rest and diversions. They suggest making time for recreation, such as hobbies and sports activities. But that advice only works for those who have the financial freedom to deliver themselves from all that is stressful.

What about people in other cultures whose idea of a good day is being able to find enough food to stay alive? And what about the families in this country who have to work hard just to make enough money for the essentials? Praise God that although we may have little or no money for diversions, we may have His peace. God's Word is for the rich and the poor. His answers don't depend on being able to circumvent circumstances.

Seeking distractions from our "stress" is very different from exulting in our tribulations. The goal of the rest, relaxation and diversion strategies is comfort. But, tribulation has another purpose—building character. The tennis court, the evening out, the vacation may be useful in our lives, but they aren't useful as a means of enabling us to bear our problems. Again, what about those who cannot afford to divert themselves with pleasantries? Is God unfair? No! He will enable us to exult in our tribulation. The circumstances have meaning. They are part of His plan. If we trust the Planner, we can trust the plan.

Stress management techniques will help us feel better, work better, accomplish more. But, we must be sure that we incorporate those techniques into the real business of our lives— allowing His Word to come alive in our hearts.

Words of Life

Offer to God a sacrifice of thanksgiving, and pay your vows to the Most High; And call upon Me in the day of trouble; I shall rescue you, and you will honor Me. (Psalm 50:14-15) You have turned for me my mourning into dancing; You have loosed my sackcloth and girded me with gladness. (Psalm 30:11) Not that I speak from want; for I have learned to be content in whatever circumstances I am. I know how to get along with humble means, and I also know how to live in prosperity; in any and every circumstance I have learned the secret of being filled and going hungry, both of having abundance and suffering need. I can do all things, through Him who strengthens me. (Philippians 4:11-13)

Living It Out

The importance of "stressful circumstances" is that they allow us to discover who we are. Remind yourself that only through the circumstances of life do we recognize our sinful nature. Recognizing our failures can be liberating! Remember too that fear and unbelief cause us to deny our sin, but when we repent and confess, we find ourselves safely in the arms of God.

Drawing From the Well of Prayer

Lord Jesus, help me to embrace my circumstances as from You. I confess and repent of any sin and of not trusting Your sovereignty and goodness. I offer You my sacrifice of thanksgiving. I will sing praise and shout for joy, even in the middle of tribulation. For then I will be renewed in the spirit of my mind to receive every blessing that You have for me through life's trials and tribulations.

Rhonda Redmon

Rhonda, the older daughter of James and Betty Robison, is married to Terry Redmon, vice president of LIFE Outreach. She homeschools their four children. Rhonda and Terry have traveled extensively on LIFE's mission trips to war- and disaster-ravaged parts of the world. She has served as a co-host on the LIFE TODAY show.

LIVING WITHOUT THE ANSWERS

One day as I was disciplining my daughter, Laney, who was six years old at the time, I sent her to her room for some "time out." I told her I would let her know when she could come out. Laney looked at me and insisted, "Mommy, you need to tell me when I can come out, because I know you're gonna forget I'm in here!" "Laney, I promise I won't forget you!" I assured her. It was obvious she did not like my answer. She began to throw a fit, crying out simply because she wanted to know when she could come out, instead of trusting that I would do it at the right time.

The minute she closed the door to her room, the Lord began to show me that this scenario with Laney was a picture of my own heart. Ever since I was a little girl, I have always been a question-asker. I'm sure my parents grew weary of the hundreds of questions I could ask in a single day! And to this day, I still have so many questions that I ask of the Lord, so many things I have yet to fully understand.

I am a diligent seeker of the truth. And while this is a great asset in my life, it can often bring me much pain. I may not throw a fit on the floor, but I can refuse to let my heart rest and trust in the Lord when I do not get an immediate answer or gain complete understanding. Often when a question comes to my mind, if I don't immediately know the answer, in some ways I stop living. My joy begins to wane and my mind becomes a circus of activity.

Proverbs 3:5-6 is a familiar verse to us all, "Trust in the Lord with all your heart and lean not on your own understanding. In all your ways acknowledge Him, and He will make your paths straight." In all your ways acknowledge Him … that means trust Him, rest in Him, even though you don't understand or even if it causes you to be angry.

The truth is that we have a Heavenly Father who loves us more than we could ever fathom. And He is more faithful to us as His children than we could ever dream of being to our own children. God has promised us that He will show us everything we need to know, that He will mold us into His image, and that He will cause the change in us. We must simply remain yielded to Him and His purposes in our lives. Sometimes, all we have to do is go to our rooms—get alone with God—and wait confidently for His answers. We can trust Him not to forget us.

Words of Life

Show me your ways, O Lord, teach me your paths; guide me in your truth and teach me, for you are God my savior, and my hope is in You all day long. Who, then, is the man that fears the Lord? He will instruct him in the way chosen for him. (Psalm 25:4-5, 12 NIV) ❧ Not by might, nor by power, but by my Spirit says the Lord Almighty. (Zechariah 4:6b) ❧ The Lord is near. Do not be anxious about anything, but in everything, by prayer and petition, with thanksgiving, present your requests (questions) to God. And the peace of God, which transcends all understanding, will guard your hearts and your minds in Christ Jesus. (Philippians 4:5-7)

Living It Out

First, if you are a parent, let God teach you many wonderful things about your relationship with Him through your children. Secondly, never allow unanswered questions to determine your level of joy. Determine not to waste hours or even days worrying about whether or not God is going to do His job! And lastly, if something needs to change in your life, trust Him to show you—but don't stop living. God is faithful, and His love for you surpasses any love you have ever known.

Drawing From the Well of Prayer

Father, speak to me today. Help me to walk in Your peace. Please guide me and teach me all that Your heart is longing for me to hear. Thank You for Your ever-increasing faithfulness to me and those I love. I trust You today—not just in the times of rejoicing—but also in the times of discipline. You are a wonderful Father to me, and I am forever grateful for Your presence in my life.

Cathy Lechner

Cathy speaks and ministers internationally, in addition to serving alongside her pastor husband, Randi. She is the author of numerous books, including *I Hope God's Promises Come to Pass Before My Body Parts Go South, I'm Trying to Sit at His Feet, but Who's Going to Cook Dinner* and *Couldn't We Just Kill 'Em and Tell God They Died?* Cathy and her husband are the parents of seven children and live in North Florida.

HUMBLE PIE ISN'T TOO BAD – IT TASTES LIKE CHICKEN

When I returned from my first missions trip, I got a firsthand look at how much religious pride was in me. On my first Sunday back home, I found myself being critical of the church. The people here had air conditioning, but did they appreciate it? Oh no! Look at everyone glancing at their watches. The poor Filipinos didn't care how long you preached; they wanted all they could get of God and His Word. In fact, most of them didn't even own a watch. On and on I judged. From the padded pews to the short and tidy sermon, I judged.

Pride is not interested in getting things done for God. Pride wants to let others know what we did and how much we did. It is totally preoccupied with our image before others.

We feel the need to let others know that God is using us just a little more than He's using someone else.

Pastor Jim Cymbala of the Brooklyn Tabernacle Church in New York City once preached what I consider to be the greatest message on the spirit of pride that I've ever heard. He made an amazing statement: "Pride has the eternal hostility of God. God resists [pride] as a general in full battle array to bring you down." This was his interpretation of 1 Peter 5:5.

When God looks down and sees pride, He smells the scent that ruined heaven, a scent very displeasing to Him. I can easily see the times in my own life that pride separated me from people I loved and ruined relationships that God had given to me. Perhaps if I had just been willing to say I'm sorry or try one more time to humble myself and change my opinions, a friendship could have been saved, an argument avoided or a situation resolved.

It's frightening when you look at Scripture and see the roll call of those who lost everything because of pride. Lucifer lost his exalted position in heaven; Nebuchadnezzar lost his kingdom; and Moses missed going into the Promised Land because of pride.

On the other hand, God gives grace to the humble. We know that grace is the unmerited favor of God, but we need to see it as the exchange we receive for our pride. Everything we need for life is contained in God's grace. As we humble ourselves, we will receive the grace that contains power, love, wisdom and the leading of God.

Words of Life

When pride comes, then comes dishonor, But with the humble is wisdom. (Proverbs 11:2)

Pride goes before destruction, and a haughty spirit before stumbling. (Proverbs 16:18)

But He gives a greater grace. Therefore it says, "God is opposed to the proud, but gives grace to the humble." (James 4:6)

Living It Out

Ask the Holy Spirit to reveal to you areas in which you have walked in pride, contention and unforgiveness. He will show you! Be quick to repent and ask for the Lord's forgiveness and the forgiveness of others if He leads you to do so. Seek Him earnestly in learning how to walk in humility and fear of the Lord.

Drawing From the Well of Prayer

Dear God, please reveal any pride in my life that hinders my relationships with other people and with You. Please replace my pride with a spirit of humility so that I may readily rejoice with others rather than judge them.

Carolyn Johnson

Carolyn is the wife of Bishop Flynn Johnson, the founder and senior elder of the Atlanta Metropolitan Cathedral in Atlanta. She is also an elder in the church, and founder/president of the Metropolitan Women's Summit. She is an accomplished vocalist, lecturer and teacher. Her emphasis is on marriage and family relationships.

AN HONEST RELATIONSHIP

Being a pastor's wife in Atlanta's inner city, I've had to frequently assume the role of mentor and mama to the young women of the area. Since most of them don't have any role models for healthy relationships, they often ask me how I am able to stay happily married for almost thirty years. Flynn and I have an excellent relationship. It is a gift from God, but we also needed to work at it.

One of the things my husband and I agreed upon a long time ago is that our relationship is only as strong as the things we are willing to talk about. What we have found over the years of being together is that if we worked on our friendship and if we fought for our friendship and a transparency between us, then the rest would come easier.

The enemy is doing all he can at this hour to destroy marriages, and we are finding that the really daring call of the Spirit of God is for couples to talk about the things they've been afraid to talk about in the past. Keeping things hidden from each other will only weaken the marriage. We need to find constructive ways to bring hard topics and feelings out in the open.

I remember one time, after twenty-three years of marriage, when I told my husband about a need that I had, I wasn't sure what his reaction would be. I said, "Flynn, I need a vacation." He said, "Great! Where should we go?" I replied, "No, you don't understand. I need a vacation by myself—without you, the children, the responsibilities of home and church … everything." Flynn was startled at first—maybe even a bit hurt. But he came around quickly and decided to wholeheartedly support me in having my need met.

Another step toward transparency is to be honest about how our monthly cycles affect us emotionally and physically. Many women have mood swings during this time that can adversely affect the marriage. I tell the men in our church, "Buy a calendar—it's one of the most powerful tools you can have." When a man know where his wife is emotionally, it helps him minister to her more effectively and saves a lot of confusion.

My husband often asks me a simple but powerful question, and it does wonders for our communication and connection. Flynn will say, "Tell me what you need me to do." I love that. It frees me up to ask him to do anything—from speaking the Word of God over me, to giving me affection without anticipation of a reward.

And finally, as you seek to develop an honest, loving relationship, remember to "fight fair" when resolving differences with your mate. This means to be truthful about your thoughts and emotions. It means to attack the issue or the action and not the person. And it means to not go to bed angry. Be mindful that even if both of you are mad, your hearts are wanting to reconnect. Be the one to reach out with honesty and humility. Your attitude will help diffuse the situation and keep your union strong.

Words of Life

The husband must fulfill his duty to his wife, and likewise also the wife to her husband. The wife does not have authority over her own body, but the husband does; and likewise also the husband does not have authority over his own body, but the wife does. Stop depriving one another, except by agreement for a time so that you may devote yourselves to prayer, and come together again so that Satan will not tempt you because of your lack of self-control. (1 Corinthians 7:3-5) And knowing their thoughts Jesus said to them, "Any kingdom divided against itself is laid waste; and any city or house divided against itself will not stand." (Matthew 12:25) An excellent wife, who can find? For her worth is far above jewels. The heart of her husband trusts in her, and he will have no lack of gain. Her children rise up and bless her;

Her husband also, and he praises her. (Proverbs 31:10-11, 28)

Living It Out

Share the thoughts from this devotion with your husband. Talk
about your desire to have a strong marriage that values honesty
and "fighting fair." Ask him if he would be willing to try to
emphasize transparent communication and resolving differences
in ways that would build up your marriage rather than tear it down.
If there are things that you've withheld from your husband that
you now feel you should share with him, ask God for wisdom and
sensitivity to do so.

Drawing From the Well of Prayer

Father God, thank You
that Your desire is for
my marriage to be strong,
honest and loving.
Please show me ways
in which I can minister
to my husband and do
all that I can to make
our home a haven.

Chonda Pierce

Chonda is known for her energetic, clean, humorous comedy routines. In fact, she's been compared to the queen of clean comedy, Minnie Pearl, but Chonda can sing too. She delivers as much vocal punch in her music as laughter for her wit. The result is her new purely music album, *Yes ... & Amen*. She has also written a book with the same title.

SMILING THROUGH THE PAIN

People often think that a Christian home—especially one in which your father is a minister—should always be stable in times of adversity. But our family saw some very dark days, and although we are not of the world, we are still in the world. And the world can sometimes be a very hard and unwelcoming place.

I was a young teenager when my sister, who was twenty years old, was suddenly killed in a tragic car accident. When Charlotta died, a deep depression settled into my dad's spirit, and he began to sink into the gloom and despair of grief.

My parents' marriage began to waiver, and they eventually divorced. Then, about twenty months after we buried Charlotta, my little sister came home from high school with a sore throat. She was fifteen, beautiful and a lot of fun. She was diagnosed with leukemia and died twenty-one days later.

My brother married and moved away shortly thereafter, so within less than a year and a half, my family of six dwindled down to just mother and me. We had to get out of the parsonage and out of the church that my dad had pastored because a new minister was coming to take his place. So, when I was eighteen, mom and I moved to a one-bedroom apartment and started life all over again.

During this time, I often heard about "God's timing" and how "time" will take care of your hurts and pain. "In time, you will feel better about this," people would say to me. I always felt like saying, "Baloney!"

For me, time never did anything about the pain. I still hurt. The tears still came. And the grief that my sisters would never know my children was all too real.

Eventually, I learned that what you let happen in the aftermath of a dark time is what makes all the difference. You can sit and wallow in the bitterness of your hour, or you can get yourself up and take your pain to the foot of the Cross—and leave it there. I found that it's possible to let go of bitterness and grab hold of joy, and even laughter, in Christ. You can either choose to let circumstances get the best of you, or you can say, "I'm going to be better for this, and move on."

I can't think of a better example of doing just that than my mother. While battling breast cancer, she began to have "no hair days" because of her chemotherapy. Wearing her new wig, one day she and I went to the cemetery to put flowers on the graves of family members. It was a very windy day. Now, nobody had told us about the tape that you can use to keep the "hair" on. The wind blew her wig right off and it rolled around wildly in the grass. I was trying to lighten the moment when I said, "Mother, you look like Yoda!" She thought it was a compliment, not having ever seen a movie in her entire life. As the hair tussled about like a tumbleweed, my poor mother yelled, "Are you going to help me catch this thing or not?" So, we chased the wig and finally caught it and shoved it back on her head. It was covered with grass and sat on top of mom's head like a crooked mess. It looked terrible.

Finally, mom was *laughing* so hard that she had to sit down to catch her breath. When she settled down, she said, "Well, as long as I can chase my hair, I guess I'm alive!" I shook my head in disbelief and thought, "Man! This has got to be the power of Jesus. Who else could come into your life at the worst moment and give you such peace that you can laugh about something that would normally break your heart?"

Words of Life

Casting all your anxiety on Him, because He cares for you. (1 Peter 5:7) 🌿 I will carry you, and I will bear you, and I will deliver you. (Isaiah 46:4b) 🌿 Cast your burden upon the Lord, and He will sustain you. (Psalm 55:22a)

Living It Out

If you are walking through a dark period, remind yourself that it's important to allow yourself time to grieve and heal. Remember that you can choose to do things that will let you say, "I'm going to be better for having gone through this." Take your pain to Jesus and ask Him to redeem it. Ask Him to send your heart on a healing journey that will result in replacing the pain with joy and even laughter. Seek wise counsel and the comfort of friends who love you.

Drawing
From the Well
of Prayer

Dear God, guide me with the light of Your love and warmth of Your comfort as I walk through this dark passage. Restore unto me the joy of Your salvation.

PART THREE: BODY

Betty Robison

Betty co-hosts the LIFE TODAY show with her husband, James Robison. She is the mother of three children and the grandmother of eleven. She has been married for over thirty-eight years and resides in the Dallas-Fort Worth area.

THREEFOLD FITNESS

I keep a watchful eye on the trends of our society. I feel a responsibility to seek a higher authority on the opinions and messages the world's authorities are offering to us. I weigh their advice in light of the Word of God. One of my greatest concerns is the way the media has drawn our focus to an extreme and impassioned emphasis on the body. The role models of magazine ads and television programs have driven the average person to strive for an unrealistic image of thinness.

I have seen what the world views as the perfect body—my mirror has prompted me to measure myself by that standard on many occasions! But God encourages me to use His measure and His image of the perfect body. He says I am "fearfully and wonderfully made" and have been created in His image. (Psalm 139:14)

God refers to our bodies as "temples of the Holy Spirit," so I conclude that He considers the care of my body to be very important. After carefully considering what I have learned from fitness and nutrition experts, I have developed a balanced maintenance plan for my body. I do this in three critical areas of my life that I have found to be vitally linked together: emotional, spiritual and physical.

Emotional—I have learned that proper care of my body can stimulate the other vital areas of my being. When I feel good physically, I become mentally and emotionally charged. If I do not take responsibility for my physical needs, I spiral down mentally and emotionally.

Spiritual—We think we are just battling cravings and laziness, but we are really in a spiritual battle for the control of our bodies. It is a spiritual battle to overrule our will and emotions when we crave foods that are bad for our bodies or we ignore our body's need for exercise. We are encouraged to "take captive every thought that exalts itself against truth." The truth is that too much of certain foods like sugar, fat and caffeine are harmful to our bodies. And the truth is that our bodies need exercise in order to stay fit.

Physical—I love to go for long, brisk walks and I target a goal of two or more miles, three to five days a week. I love to walk with a friend because it gives me great fellowship and encouragement on my journey to total fitness. If I am walking alone, I converse with the Lord and listen as He tells me all the things that "pertain to life and godliness" for me, my family and my ministry.

Words of Life

Beloved, I pray that in all respects you may prosper and be in good health, just as your soul prospers. (3 John 1:2)

Additional Reading:

1 Corinthians 6:12-20

1 Corinthians 15:40-58

Living It Out

There is a wealth of good information available to help us make good nutritional choices as well as proper exercise choices. Do some research or see your doctor to make sure you have a good idea of how to eat and exercise properly for your age and weight. Make some personal goals in the areas of physical, emotional and spiritual health. Find a "threefold fitness" partner who will encourage you on the road to reaching your goals.

Drawing From the Well of Prayer

Father, I know You want me to honor You with my body. I want to be Your temple of holiness— to exercise self-control so that my body is strong and healthy. I want to walk in the energy and power of Your Holy Spirit. Help me to take every thought captive to the obedience of Christ and make the best choices for my emotional, physical and spiritual health.

Sheri Rose Shepherd

Sheri Rose speaks on freedom from dieting and emotional distress through the Bible. She is the author of several books, including *Fit for Excellence, Who Would Have Thought, Life Is Not a Dress Rehearsal,* and *7 Ways to Build a Better You.* She resides with her husband, Steve, and their two children in Oregon.

FIT FOR EXCELLENCE

I used to travel through life in two gears: park and fifth. I managed to strip all the others. I would push myself past the highest speed limits known to man, ignoring the big yellow warning lights screaming, "Slow down! Stop! Rest!" I found myself saying yes to any and every opportunity that seemed like a good cause— even if I wasn't called or equipped to do it!

I ignored my body's cry for rest. I was thrown out on the road of reality when my body completely shut down during a speaking engagement. There I was, speaking about spiritual excellence as I fell over on the floor! (No, I was not slain in the Spirit!)

I was diagnosed with chronic fatigue syndrome. My immune system had completely shut down. I was so exhausted that I could hardly lift my head off the pillow. The doctor informed me that I would have to stop all activity—in other words, pull my lifestyle out of fifth gear and put it in park.

Every day as I lay in bed, I'd cry. I didn't get to play with my little boy, go to church, or go out with my friends. I missed ministering. I begged God to show me if there was any way to heal my body.

I began to research and compare differences between biblical diets and the modern American diet. I found that the biblical diet consisted mainly of raw fruits and vegetables, raw seeds, whole grains, and occasional meats and fish. (See Genesis 1:29.) I was shocked to find that most of the things I was eating weren't really food at all and had little or no nutritional value.

I decided to put the biblical diet to the test. I cut out all white flour, white sugar, processed food, artificial sweeteners, caffeine, dairy products and tap water. Giving up the "trash foods" I had grown to love was the hardest battle I'd ever fought against my flesh, because no matter where I turned it was hard to escape these foods.

It was a battle worth winning. In eight weeks I was able to lose the twenty-three pounds I had gained lying in bed, I conquered my chronic fatigue, and I entered the Mrs. USA pageant and won the crown! My skin looked healthy, my hair thickened, and my energy level was incredible.

Today, I am so thankful that my body taught me how to listen to the Lord.

Words of Life

Do you not know that you are a temple of God and that the Spirit of God dwells in you? If any man destroys the temple of God, God will destroy him, for the temple of God is holy, and that is what you are. (1 Corinthians 3:16-17) Or do you not know that your body is a temple of the Holy Spirit who is in you, whom you have from God, and that you are not your own? (1 Corinthians 6:19) Therefore I urge you, brethren, by the mercies of God, to present your bodies a living and holy sacrifice, acceptable to God, which is your spiritual service of worship. And do not be conformed to this world, but be transformed by the renewing of your mind, so that you may prove what the will of God is, that which is good and acceptable and perfect. (Romans 12:1-2)

Living It Out

Identify the root of your food addictions or overeating. Find an accountability partner to pray with you and be a continual source of encouragement. Don't bring foods into your home that will be tempting. Try to exercise at least twenty minutes every day. Make time in your schedule to prepare healthy foods to keep on hand. Try to stop eating after 7 p.m. And finally, when you stick to your plan each day, reward yourself with something fun or exciting that you really enjoy, like a bubble bath, renting a great movie, making a fire in the fireplace, or talking with a girlfriend on the phone for an hour.

Drawing From the Well of Prayer

Dear God, help me to see that my body is Your temple. Give me the strength to make the right choices in my daily eating habits. Please shift my focus on dieting from one of denial to one of opportunity—to focus on all the great things I'll be able to do when I remain healthy and feel good about myself.

Linda Weber

Linda is the author of *Mom, You're Incredible!* and *Women of Splendor*. She is the mother of three married sons. She and her husband, Stu, also an author, have led FamilyLife Marriage and Parenting conferences for Campus Crusade for Christ and have ministered to military groups and churches across the country. She has also appeared on the *700 Club*.

BEAUTY–
INSIDE AND OUT

I grew up in a conservative church where we were not taught physical ways to enhance beauty. Outward appearance was downplayed, and only abstract spiritual qualities were considered worthy of developing.

As a little girl, I remember watching the Miss America pageant and thinking how beautiful those women were. Although I didn't possess the raw material to pursue such titles, I mentally cast myself into the fairy-tale role of being one of those poised and talented finalists. I longed to develop that feminine aura, which I saw so beautifully presented.

Many of us receive mixed messages about how Christian women should view physical beauty. In *The Woman Behind the Mirror*, Judith Couchman writes, "I've needed to celebrate the God-endowed face and body that is uniquely and utterly mine." I heartily agree that we need to remember that there is a physical side to being spiritual.

The body is an incredible design of God. Daily we have the privilege to make the most of what we've been given. Maintenance is a biblical principle that applies in every area of life. We would never buy a house or car and not take care of it. We spend money on preventing problems, on insurance in case things come up and on repairs as needs arise.

In the same way, God gives us a body and expects us to maintain it. We take precautions by eating the right foods and avoiding unhealthy ones. We exercise and even "pump iron." (Proverbs 31:17 says, "She girds herself with strength, And makes her arms strong.") We discipline ourselves to get adequate sleep. These are the basics.

To go beyond the basics, it's interesting to note that "The Proverbs 31 Lady" had clothing of fine linen and purple. And 1 Peter 3:3 takes for granted the expression of external beauty, mentioning the woman's braided hair and her wearing of gold jewelry and fine dresses. Where inner development is obviously essential, there is an assumption that the externals were cared for.

Consequently, looking good to please God is biblical. Contentedness in pleasing Him will nullify any body hatred, such as the fear of looking old, or trends of anorexia, bulimia or other unhealthy obsessions. Living out a God-focused life ensures your body is in order.

Creating beauty as a designer for God is a worthwhile mission. There is theology to it all, for "whatever you do, do all to the glory of God." Acquiring even small tips will help you do justice to the body you have been given—tips regarding:

- Face shapes and the best way to cut and style your hair
- Seasonal coloring of your skin tone,

    for making better choices of colors to use or wear
- Body sizes and shapes,

    to minimize and maximize needed areas with clothing choices.

Don't forget to praise God for the body with which He has blessed you. Enhancing and appreciating this outward beauty in a healthy way glorifies Him through beauty that dwells within.

Words of Life

Whatever you do, do all to the glory of God. (1 Corinthians 10:31) ❧ She makes coverings for herself; Her clothing is fine linen and purple. (Proverbs 31:22) ❧ Your body is a temple of the Holy Spirit. (1 Corinthians 6:19)

Living It Out

Read Proverbs 31 and Peter 3:3. These scriptures reinforce the concept that there is a physical side to spiritual beauty. Take a personal inventory of things about your body and appearance that you would like to enhance. Read books or magazines that will offer beauty and fashion tips. Talk with a friend or someone you admire who may be able to share some fun insights on how to make the most of your appearance. Work on making desired changes in the coming weeks.

Drawing From the Well of Prayer

Father, I thank You for the unique body and face You have given me. Help me to enhance Your gifts, both inward and outward, and use them all for Your glory.

Susan Negus, Ph.D.

Susan has her doctorate in holistic health. She has done research in nutrition, herbs, physiology, and homeopathy. She is on the Board of Directors for the American Holistic Health Association.

DYING TO LIVE

A few years ago, I was diagnosed with lupus, a debilitating disease that was literally draining the life out of me. I had to pray every day to get out of bed—it took all the energy that I had. But I knew if I didn't get out of bed every morning, I might not ever get out of bed again. I knew that I had a year or two to live at the most. I made the decision that I wanted to live. So, I prayed and then I took action.

I started by going to a naturopathic doctor and choosing to change my lifestyle. I altered my eating habits, got on a nutritional supplement program and eventually started exercising. The most important lesson I learned through this experience was that, just as I had to feed my spirit every day and take care of it, I had to do the same for my body.

Have you ever said, "I wish I knew what to do about my allergies, or weight problem, or headaches or blemishes, etc.?" Well, the good news is that there are many steps you can take toward healthy living. It will take some discipline, but your willingness to give up some of the habits and foods that are bad for you and substitute them for good habits and foods will result in a healthier body and, more importantly, prepare you for God's service.

A good place to start is to choose foods that are in their most natural state when you go to the grocery store. That means buying the freshest fruits and vegetables you can find, as well as fresh lean meat, chicken and fish. Avoid foods that have been heavily processed, colored or preserved with chemical additives.

Make an effort to get proper exercise. Inactivity can rob your body (which has 600 muscles that need exercise) of the strength and endurance you need to do the work God has given you. Consult a health care professional before beginning any exercise program, but the important thing is to begin.

Maintain a positive mental attitude by filling your mind with the Word of God. Be careful what you allow into your mind through television and popular culture. Purpose to yield worry and doubt to the Lord, for He cares for you.

Make prayer a way of life. Confide in the Lord about all that is good, bad or confusing. Give Him your cares and trust Him to meet your needs. Listen to the Lord and submit to His leading in your life.

Cultivate at least one or two close friendships. Good friends will encourage you when life is tough and help you learn to laugh at yourself. Spend time with people who bless and encourage you.

Learn more about God's love and faithfulness. Your love for God will grow and lead to a deeper love for others. Ask the Lord to help you see others in a new light and seek to bless them through prayer, patience and simple acts of kindness.

And finally, if you truly want to be a healthy, happy Christian, it's important to accept the fact that God knows what is best for you. Your willingness to accept His love and lordship will help you see submission as an adventure in grace, not a dreaded duty.

Here's to a healthier, happier you!

Words of Life

Therefore I urge you, brethren, by the mercies of God, to present your bodies a living and holy sacrifice, acceptable to God, which is your spiritual service of worship. (Romans 12:1) ❧ But if any of you lacks wisdom, let him ask of God, who gives to all believers generously and without reproach, and it will be given to him. (James 1:5) ❧ And do not be conformed to this world, but be transformed by the renewing of your mind, so that you may prove what the will of God is, that which is good and acceptable and perfect. (Romans 12:2)

Living It Out

Just as God speaks to you through your spirit, He also speaks

through your body. Your body will tell you what it needs. But you

have to listen, because it's when we don't listen that things start

falling apart. A journey toward health should follow a plan that

produces a healthy spirit and mind, as well as a stronger body.

The key is balance, and the result is wholeness in every area of

your life. Ask the Lord to give you strength to honor the life He

has given you by taking care of yourself—body, mind and spirit.

Drawing From the Well of Prayer

Dear Lord, give me the strength to honor the life You have given me. Help me to take good care of my body, to fill my mind with good things and to nourish my spirit by walking in Your presence.

Linda Mintle, Ph.D.

Linda is a psychotherapist who writes for *Charisma*, *Spirit Led Woman* and *Ministries Today* magazines. She has co-hosted the *700 Club*. She is the author of a number of books, including *Getting Unstuck*, a book dealing with women's issues.

FREEDOM FROM FOOD

Weight matters to women. No matter how emotionally healthy you think you are, you still obsess a little about your weight. Admit it. When you try on bathing suits in the spring, isn't it a little depressing? Have you lied about your weight on your driver's license? Are you dieting because of a wedding, class reunion or special event?

And what about those yearly physicals when the nurse weighs us? We make certain that our shoes are off (that's another two pounds), our watch (gotta be worth a few ounces) or earrings (a few more ounces), and our jacket (easily a pound). Stripped to the lowest common denominator—a flimsy lightweight dress over underwear—we pray the scale will be kind.

Who can we thank for our corporal neurosis? Lots of

people, actually—our culture, our race and ethnicity, our socioeconomic status, ourselves, our families and our biology. Our weight is influenced by all these things.

The reality for most of us is we don't look like the *Sports Illustrated* models in a bathing suit, and we probably never will. For all the money spent on weight loss, we have epidemic rates of obesity. Why in a society so health-and-fitness conscious are we still so fat?

A part of the reason is that we eat tons of processed food, much of it high in fat and loaded with empty calories. We exercise very little and spend much of our leisure time in front of screens—movies, TV and computers.

For some women, food becomes a friend and is used to fill emotional voids. Binge and compulsive eaters have often faced numerous losses in their lives (divorce, neglect, abuse, alcoholic parents, rejection and loneliness), and they use food to soothe and protect themselves from pain.

Food is an available object that gives pleasure and is often used to calm anxiety, cover anger, protect from sexual issues and much more. Food is often equated with love. If you experience a lack of love, you can fill yourself with food. Food fills the empty places. Food obsessions keep us stuck. Instead of dealing with life's losses and voids directly, we are distracted with food.

My advice is simple, but it is incredibly hard to do: Learn to eat sensibly, begin to exercise and stop using food as your emotional nurturer. Spiritually, fill yourself up so that food takes on less power in your life. You do not need to be a slave to food. You may have to work with a therapist to make this happen.

God's love produces self-control. Because we love God, we want to please Him. As we bring ourselves into obedience to His way of living our lives, these things produce self-discipline. This may mean changing your behavior and addressing areas you have previously denied or numbed by food.

So work on all your "stuff" associated with overeating but don't neglect filling yourself up with God's Word. It produces love, which produces self-control. God's love is the secret ingredient. It's what changes us from striving to overcoming!

Words of Life

Therefore if any man is in Christ, he is a new creature; the old things passed away; behold, new things have come. (2 Corinthians 5:17) Submit therefore to God. Resist the devil and he will flee from you. (James 4:7) But the fruit of the Spirit is love, joy, peace, patience, kindness, goodness, faithfulness, gentleness, self-control; against such things there is no law. (Galatians 5:22-23)

Living It Out

Ask God to show you how you are using food. Confide in a friend or a counselor and brainstorm ways in which those needs can be met without using food. Buy a healthy cookbook and educate yourself about eating sensibly. Determine to exercise at least thirty minutes, three days a week—even if it's just taking a brisk walk.

Drawing From the Well of Prayer

Dear God, I want to please You and I want to stop being distracted by my weight and overeating. Please help me to hide Your Word in my heart so that I might make healthier choices for my body and spirit. Thank You that I don't have to be a slave to food and that You will give me the perseverance to make whatever changes are necessary to gain freedom from food issues.

Debra
Evans

Debra's expertise is in the area of health and wellness. She is an author, teacher, conference speaker, and presenter on pro-life and medical ethics. She has done over 200 radio interviews, has appeared on television, and has written many articles for popular magazines.

LOVING YOUR BODY– A KEY TO HEALTHY SEXUALITY

I have never been able to remain quiet about my amazement at God's handiwork, the human body. I am continually fascinated by its complex intricacies. Whenever I witness a newborn infant taking a first breath of air, I still can hardly believe that the baby I am looking at began just nine short months ago as two microscopic cells.

Isaac Newton once noted, "In the absence of any other proof, the thumb alone would convince me of God's existence." Have you, like this famous physicist, ever stopped to ponder how the complexity and wisdom of God are reflected in your wondrous design? Do you accept your physical beauty and praise God for the wonder of your body's intricate structure, head to toe, inside and outside, seen and unseen?

Something beautiful happens when a woman lets go of the fear, shame and anxiety she feels about the way she looks and accepts her body, rich with imperfection, as a gift of God. When she stops despising certain aspects of her appearance—her wide hips, pesky cellulite, double chin, droopy abdomen, small breasts or bony backside—and smiles at the imperfect reflection in the mirror.

Our attitudes about the way our bodies look have a powerful impact on the way we think and feel about our self-worth and our sexuality. We must remember that our spiritual value does not reside in our bodies, which the apostle Paul aptly called "jars of clay." It lies in the glorious treasure God has placed inside these earthly vessels. *Our bodies deserve our tender loving care rather than our constant criticism and contempt.*

As we learn about our bodies, we are more likely to take good care of them. When we take the time to discover how our bodies work, we are also better able to talk about the sexual sensations and experiences we have. Through understanding what is happening inside our bodies, communicating with our spouses takes on greater importance. We are more likely to place a higher value on talking about the things that please, bother, surprise, irritate and excite us.

When a woman learns to appreciate her body with the humor and grace God alone can give, she warmly welcomes her husband with her body. This is key to experiencing happy sexuality and a marriage that thrives in the way the Lord intended it to.

Words of Life

For You formed my inward parts; You wove me in my mother's womb. I will give thanks to You, for I am fearfully and wonderfully made; Wonderful are Your works, And my soul knows it very well. (Psalm 139:13-14) ❧ My beloved is mine, and I am his; I am my beloved's, and his desire is for me. (Song of Solomon 2:16a, 7:10) ❧ The wife does not have authority over her own body, but the husband does; and likewise also the husband does not have authority over his own body, but the wife does. (1 Corinthians 7:4)

Living It Out

Make a point in the coming weeks to learn at least one new thing about your body that relates to your sexuality. Buy a book or teaching tape that encourages a healthy body image and sexual fulfillment in marriage. Determine to be honest with your husband about the positive and negative sexual feelings and experiences you have. And finally, pray for God's blessing on your sexual relationship.

Drawing From the Well of Prayer

God be in my head and

in my understanding;

God be in my eyes

and in my looking;

God be in my mouth

and in my speaking;

God be in my heart

and in my thinking.

Anonymous

SOURCES

Lisa Bevere: *You Are Not What You Weigh* (Creation House, Orlando, 1998), pp. 27-35, 43-44, 46, 50, 146-147.
Interview on LIFE TODAY's show, *Another View*, 2000.

Anita Bryant: *A New Day: A Triumphant Story of Forgiveness, Healing and Recovery* (Anita Bryant Publishing, 1996), pp. 19-28.
For more information, contact Anita Bryant, P.O. Box 560, Sevierville, TN 37862. 865.908.2727.

Esther Burroughs: *Splash the Living Water: Turning Daily Interruptions Into Life-Giving Encounters* (Thomas Nelson Publishers, Nashville, 1999), pp. 7, 139-166. Used by permission of Thomas Nelson Publishers.
Interviews on LIFE TODAY.

Valorie Burton: *Rich Minds, Rich Rewards* (Pearl Books, Dallas, 1999), pp. 51-57.
Interview on LIFE TODAY's show, *Another View*, 2000.

Terry Dorian: *Health Begins in Him* (Huntington House Publishers, Lafayette, 1995), pp. 68-73.

Debra Evans: *The Christian Woman's Guide to Sexuality* (Crossway Book, Wheaton, 1997), pp. 37-41, 274.
Interview on LIFE TODAY's show, *Pathway to Intimacy*.

Carolyn Johnson: Interview on LIFE TODAY.

Ellie Kay: *Shop, Save, and Share* (Bethany House Publishers, Minneapolis, 1998), pp. 181-184.

Anna Kendall: *Speaking of Love* (Family Restoration Network, Dallas, Texas, 1995), pp. 61-63.

Carol Kent: *Becoming a Woman of Influence: Making a Lasting Impact on Others* (Navpress, Colorado Springs, 1999), pp. 166-170.

Cathy Lechner: *Couldn't We Just Kill 'Em and Tell God They Died?* (Creation House, 1997), pp. 52-55.

Linda Mintle: *Getting Unstuck* (Creation House, Lake Mary, 1999), pp. 229-270.
Interview on LIFE TODAY's show, *Another View, 2000.*

Susan Negus: *A Better Life* (LIFE Outreach International, Fort Worth, 2000), pp. 5-7.
Interviews on LIFE TODAY.

Stormie Omartian: *Finding Peace for Your Heart: A Woman's Guide to Emotional Health* (Thomas Nelson Publishers, Nashville, 1991), pp. 246-265. Used by permission of Thomas Nelson Publishers.

Chonda Pierce: Interviews on LIFE TODAY.

Ann Pretorius: Original submission.

Rhonda Redmon: Original submission.

Betty Robison: Original submissions.

Jeanne Rogers: Original submission.

Sheri Rose Shepherd: *Fit for Excellence: God's Design for Spiritual, Emotional & Physical Health* (Creation House, Orlando, 1998), pp. 84-86 & 91.

Rebecca St. James: *You're the Voice: 40 More Days With God* (Thomas Nelson Publishers, Nashville, 1997), pp. 31 & 32. Used by permission of Thomas Nelson Publishers.

Luci Swindoll: *You Bring the Confetti, God Brings the Joy* (Word Publishing, Nashville, 1997), pp. 100-101, 105-112.

Becky Tirabassi: *Change Your Life: Achieve a Healthy Body, Heal Relationships & Connect With God* (G. P. Putnam's Sons, New York, 2001), pp. 88-97.
For more information, please contact Becky Tirabassi Change Your Life, Inc., P.O. Box 9672, Newport Beach, CA 92660. 800.444.6189. www.changeyourlifedaily.com.

Robin Turner: Original submission.

Sheila Walsh: *Honestly* (Zondervan Publishing House, Grand Rapids, 1996), pp. 68-79.
Interview on LIFE TODAY.

Linda Weber: *Woman of Splendor: Discovering the Four Facets of Godly Woman* (Broadman & Holman Publishers, Nashville, 1999), pp. 192-200.

Thelma Wells: *Girl, Have I Got Good News For You* (Thomas Nelson Publishers, Nashville, 2000). Used by permission of Thomas Nelson Publishers.

Martha Williamson: *Inviting God to Your Wedding* (Random House, New York, 2000), pp. 81-83.

CeCe Winans: *On a Positive Note* (Pocket Books, New York, 1999), pp. 196-204.

A Ministry of LIFE Outreach International

In USA:
Post Office Box 982000
Fort Worth, Texas 76182

In Canada:
Post Office Box 4000
Langley, BC V3A 8J8

1-800-947-LIFE (5433)
www.lifetoday.org